SAVA[I]

Food Crawls

Jesse Blanco

TOURING *the* **NEIGHBORHOODS**
ONE BITE *&* **LIBATION** *at a* **TIME**

Globe
Pequot

ESSEX, CONNECTICUT

Globe Pequot

An imprint of Globe Pequot, the trade division of
The Rowman & Littlefield Publishing Group, Inc.
4501 Forbes Blvd., Ste. 200
Lanham, MD 20706
www.rowman.com

Distributed by NATIONAL BOOK NETWORK

British Library Cataloguing in Publication Information available

Library of Congress Cataloging-in-Publication Data

Names: Blanco, Jesse, author.
Title: Savannah food crawls : touring the neighborhoods one bite & libation at a time / Jesse Blanco.
Description: Essex, Connecticut : Globe Pequot, [2023] | Series: Food crawls | Includes index.
Identifiers: LCCN 2022049237 (print) | LCCN 2022049238 (ebook) | ISBN 9781493058846 (paperback) | ISBN 9781493058853 (epub)
Subjects: LCSH: Restaurants—Georgia—Savannah—Guidebooks. | Bars (Drinking establishments)—Georgia—Savannah—Guidebooks. | Savannah (Ga.)—Guidebooks.
Classification: LCC TX907.3.G42 S284 2023 (print) | LCC TX907.3.G42 (ebook) | DDC 647.95758231--dc23/eng/20221214
LC record available at https://lccn.loc.gov/2022049237
LC ebook record available at https://lccn.loc.gov/2022049238

∞™ The paper used in this publication meets the minimum requirements of American National Standard for Information Sciences—Permanence of Paper for Printed Library Materials, ANSI/NISO Z39.48-1992

Contents

Foreword

WHEN I WAS A CHILD AND ABLE TO RIDE ON THE CENTER armrest of our 1953 Buick Super unbelted and occasionally allowed to "drive" sitting in my father's lap with all our four hands on the steering wheel, dining in Savannah seemed, in today's view, limited.

For seafood, there was Williams' Seafood on Tybee Road, along the Bull River. It was a Sunday specialty, especially for fried shrimp, fried fish, deviled crab, oysters—all of it—for one's family.

Gottlieb's Bakery was another staple, and on Sundays after church we loved to get water rolls, which were always warm, from Joe, Irving, Elliott, and Sadie Gottlieb. We'd also visit them at their deli a few years later, where the Gottliebs would provide the glacé fruit that we added to our tutti-frutti ice cream.

There was also barbecue. Walls' BBQ made some of the best down-home food, including BBQ, in town. Johnny Harris was another Sunday place and date haven. Hester's Martinique had a novalike existence downtown with great steaks and candlelit dinners. And for a really fancy evening, there was the Rex on East Broad.

The Boar's Head came along in the early 1960s with the emergence of River Street popularity, well before there was a paved street or Rousakis Plaza. This was when the train still ran to the plants on the east side and, on occasion, the engineer would enter the Port Royal Cafe where we teens would sometimes congregate, and ask us to move our cars so his train could pass. Shortly after that Spanky's, with its original chicken fingers, and Some Place Else, another popular restaurant and bar, arrived. There was the Savoy Cafe on Whitaker for the late-night Damon Runyonesque denizens of Savannah and Anton's on the west side of Broughton Street. Ah, the pastries that Heinz turned out for the owner Andy Andris are remembered!

Tassey Salas, who was a nephew of the Andrises, a longtime Savannah restaurant family, was the maître d' at Anton's and later opened Tassey's Pier in Thunderbolt, which brought international attention to Savannah in the 1970s and '80s. During that time, the city began to diversify in the culinary world.

Donna Moeckel opened the Italian-inspired, fine dining establishment Garibaldi and reimagined the Olde Pink House several years later when she purchased it with her family. Around the same time, Elizabeth Terry at Elizabeth on 37th, and Sema Wilkes of Mrs. Wilkes Boarding House, became Savannah's earliest James Beard Award winners.

Following, an array of restaurants like Paula Deen's the Lady & Sons, Olympia Cafe, Alligator Soul, Jazz'd, and many others appeared in the 1990s and early 2000s, earning national accolades. Downtown was reawakening.

Since then, the emergence of a vibrant restaurant scene throughout downtown Savannah has driven a culinary expansion through midtown, Southside, the Starland District, and surrounding neighborhoods like Wilmington Island and Tybee Island.

Savannah is now a "foodie" town, a destination driven by culinary vision-aries like the Grey's Mashama Bailey, who earned this year's coveted James Beard Outstanding Chef title, and Cheryl Day of Back in the Day Bakery, both of whom are becoming household names.

It's an especially exciting time in Savannah's modern history.

Through all the years and all the fine victuals there was always our ice cream . . . a sweet choice in Savannah since 1919!

—Stratton Leopold, Leopold's Ice Cream

Introduction

WELCOME TO SAVANNAH! WHILE SAVANNAH'S STORIED HISTORY dates all the way back to 1733, and there has been a lot of good food here for decades, this city's culinary renaissance began in earnest In 2014. In the big picture, a very short time ago.

In 2014 we saw a flurry of restaurants first open their doors in pretty rapid succession. Restaurants that to this day are some of the best and most popular in the city. Long known for our comfort food and Southern classics, this renaissance began to provide Savannah with culinary diversity never before seen in this area.

For the better part of the last decade, talented chefs have come to Savannah from all over America both to learn the "Southern" way of cooking, which dates back centuries, and also move some of those flavors in a modern direction. That's to say nothing of the talent that was already here. There is plenty of it, and we have been the beneficiaries of their passion and skill.

Downtown Savannah's open container laws allow us to walk our city streets with any beverage of choice in our hand. That fact alone makes Savannah very alcohol forward. No, it's not all we do, but we do it openly as well as responsibly. For that reason, you will find a lot of great choices in the beverage department on our crawls, but the primary focus is to eat well and we will.

When you come to Savannah, you had better show up hungry.

Follow the Icons

 If you eat something outrageous and don't take a photo for Instagram, did you really eat it? These restaurants feature dishes that are Instagram famous. These foods must be seen (and snapped) to be believed, and luckily, they taste as good as they look!

 This icon means that sweet treats are ahead. Bring your sweet tooth to these spots for dessert first (or second or third).

 Cheers to a fabulous night out in Savannah! These spots add a little glam to your grub and are perfect for marking a special occasion.

 Follow this icon when you're crawling for cocktails. This symbol points out the establishments that are best known for their great drinks. The food never fails here, but be sure to come thirsty too!

THE PLANT RIVERSIDE DISTRICT CRAWL

1. **BAOBAB LOUNGE,** JW MARRIOTT, 400 W. RIVER ST., SAVANNAH, (912) 373-9033, PLANTRIVERSIDE.COM/VENUES/BAOBAB-LOUNGE/

2. **GRAFFITO,** POWER PLANT BUILDING AT PLANT RIVERSIDE DISTRICT, SAVANNAH, (912) 373-9060, PLANTRIVERSIDE.COM/VENUES/GRAFFITO/

3. **STONE AND WEBSTER CHOPHOUSE,** POWER PLANT BUILDING AT PLANT RIVERSIDE DISTRICT, SAVANNAH, (912) 373-9066, PLANTRIVERSIDE.COM/VENUES/STONE-WEBSTER-CHOPHOUSE

4. **DISTRICT GELATO,** THREE MUSES BUILDING AT PLANT RIVERSIDE DISTRICT, SAVANNAH, (912) 373-9100, PLANTRIVERSIDE.COM/VENUES/DISTRICT-GELATO/

5. **MYRTLE & ROSE,** ROOFTOP GARDEN, THREE MUSES BUILDING AT PLANT RIVERSIDE DISTRICT, SAVANNAH, (912) 373-9080, PLANTRIVERSIDE.COM/VENUES/MYRTLE-ROSE-ROOFTOP-GARDEN

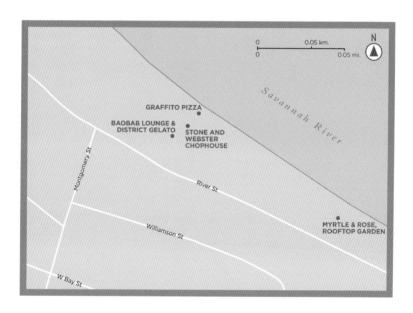

Plant Riverside District

Savannah's Modern-Day Theme Park

Built on the extreme western end of Savannah's famed River Street, the Plant Riverside District is our city's shiny new penny. Anchored by the JW Marriott Hotel, the sprawling complex is composed of three riverfront buildings, each featuring a different theme. The two main buildings in the center are an impeccably restored power plant. The plant provided power for Savannah from 1912 until it was decommissioned in 2005.

Rising above the hotel are twin 176-foot smokestacks that have already become a part of Savannah's historic skyline. The hotel's massive atrium features a natural science exhibit and activities for children.

In and around the complex you will find more than a dozen food and beverage venues ranging from Starbucks Coffee, housemade gelatos, and pizza all the way up to Savannah's best local steakhouse, Stone and Webster. District Seafood and District Smokehouse both feature long bars of outdoor seating where you can enjoy a snack or a beverage about 100 feet from the railing and the Savannah River. Savannah Tequila Company is its Mexican food outlet, featuring one of the largest tequila selections in Savannah.

1

BAOBAB LOUNGE

Highlighted by "raw elements with modern elegance," **BAOBAB** may be one of the most ornate "lobby bars" in Savannah. Located just off the JW Marriott Hotel's lobby, it is the perfect spot to begin a stroll across the complex. The space is dedicated to African cultures honoring the origins of humankind.

With wines, cocktails, and a collection of small plates, Baobab has made a strong push as my favorite place for a few bites in the building. The harissa steak flatbread has been on the menu since day one and with good reason. Vegetarians can enjoy the roasted beet hummus. On the cocktail side, meanwhile, the Starbucks lovers in your group will absolutely enjoy the Mazagran: Irish whiskey, Madagascar vanilla syrup, French-pressed chilled coffee, and coffee bean–infused Angostura. You'll swear you just picked it up at the mobile order station, until that Irish whiskey kicks in. Or maybe the Bull of the Serengeti: vodka, blueberry Red Bull, lemon juice, simple syrup, and Fee Brothers Fee foam.

A REVITALIZED RIVERFRONT!

The Plant Riverside District broke ground in December 2016 and took over 4 years to complete. When the grand opening was held in the summer of 2020, the Atlantic building was unfinished. It features the properties' only swimming pool, on the roof, and opened over a year later.

2
GRAFFITO

Making your way across the hotel's lobby, you will make your way past Stone and Webster Chophouse (we'll be circling back there shortly). Next to the steakhouse you will see the base of one of the complex's famed smokestacks. Yes, they are real. Yes, they were used when this building produced electricity for most of the city.

Out the doors you will get your first peek at the Savannah River just ahead. A few hundred feet to the right you will arrive at Graffito Pizza, Plant Riverside's Neapolitan pizzeria.

When they opened, **GRAFFITO** was among the best pizza in the city. Since then, we've had a few new pizzerias open across Savannah, but Graffito remains one of my go-tos when I am in the area.

The space is as colorful as you will find in all of Savannah. It is dominated by an authentic graffiti mural created by Atlanta-based street artist Greg Mike. The colorful atmosphere will make Graffito appealing to the kids, yes, but then so will the food. Neapolitan pizzas are the calling card here with twin wood-burning ovens on one side of the room. That is not to say the other menu items aren't equally as tasty. The meatballs al forno are made with pork and veal and then topped with marinara and ricotta and finished with a generous snowfall of freshly grated parmigiano. They are delicious.

I've never had a pizza here I did not enjoy. Quattro formaggi (four cheese) is always a hit, but their standard margherita should not be overlooked. There is a varied selection of pies for every taste. They also feature a selection of salads and pastas. All of it accompanied by a beer and wine list as well as a full liquor bar.

3

STONE AND WEBSTER CHOPHOUSE

For all the culinary diversity you will find while visiting Savannah, the classic American steakhouse is a niche that had escaped us until **STONE AND WEBSTER** opened here at the Plant Riverside District. Yes, you can find a variety of steakhouse franchises in Savannah, but S&W is the only independent steakhouse. Which matters in my book. Because of that, they have developed a good following with locals.

You'll find Stone and Webster (named for the engineering firm that helped design the original power plant in 1912) inside PRD's main building. Reservations are highly recommended here. If you are a steakhouse connoisseur like I am, then you know the drill. You can enjoy a shrimp cocktail or maybe some oysters to start you off, but my go-to starter here is the pork belly confit. Made

As big as the JW Marriott in the **Plant Riverside District** is, it is only 16 rooms larger than Savannah's next-largest hotel, the Westin Savannah Harbor: 419 to 403.

with black garlic, green garlic, and farro verde.

The beef overall is good, but the treasures here are on the very short (and always changing) "Butcher's Reserve" list. On one visit, I enjoyed a wagyu skirt steak from this list. It was among the best I've ever had. The sides, including potatoes a few different ways as well as a few vegetables, are all good. The accompaniments, like blue cheese fondue and black truffle butter, shouldn't be overlooked.

Of course you can enjoy a classic dessert here, or you can save that portion of your appetite for one of our last two stops, which I would recommend.

4 DISTRICT GELATO

With a complex this big and Savannah summers being what they are, you are obviously going to find more than one spot at PRD to satisfy your sweet tooth. Savannah's Byrd Cookie Company is a national brand but remains family owned and operated right here in Savannah. Their cookies are exceptional. Their shop here at PRD is always a worthwhile stop, but it's hard to pass on something ice cold when the temperatures are pushing triple digits.

DISTRICT GELATO is Plant Riverside's "ice cream shop." Of course, now we are wondering what the difference is, right? There are a number of different ways to explain it, but it all comes down to how they are made and, generally, gelato does not contain egg yolks.

All of that aside, the gelato at District Gelato is all made on the premises, which absolutely makes a difference. Here you will find 2 dozen or so different flavors to be enjoyed as scoops or even sundaes and milkshakes. There is no indoor seating here. It is basically grab and go with gelato scooped to order, but then you need to talk about how delicious it is while you are walking away.

There is some outdoor seating near District Gelato, but it is also seating for the general population visiting PRD. So you may grab a seat, but you may not. The good news is, either way you will have a perfect view of the Savannah River.

5

MYRTLE & ROSE, ROOFTOP GARDEN

A lot of factors go into the making of a perfect rooftop venue. Of course, you need a view. You need a solid selection of beverages, and you need a good vibe. Good food is always a plus, but not necessary from my seat, which is part of the reason why I enjoy **MYRTLE & ROSE** as much as I do.

Myrtle & Rose is one of two rooftop venues at the Plant Riverside District, the other being Electric Moon. Each spot wisely targets a different demographic, but not at the expense of either when it comes to offering an engaging experience. Electric Moon features an outdoor play area and a slide from one level to the next. It's also the spot you are most likely to see a group lining up shots of Fireball or a bachelorette party in matching attire "woo-hooing" their way across Savannah.

Myrtle & Rose, conversely, is a little lower on the octane. That is not to say that you won't see any of what I described above at Myrtle & Rose, but it is less likely. How do they describe it? Inspired by the flowers used in the crowns often worn by muses in classical mythology, this rooftop garden is named for Myrtle and Rose, symbols of femininity, love, and romance. Yes, that.

It is stunningly beautiful and offers arguably the best view of the Savannah River of any rooftop not named Lost Square (which is at the Alida Hotel).

The venue is tough to beat at Myrtle & Rose. On Sundays they offer a three-piece jazz brunch. Every other day or night, it is the perfect spot to end a tour of Savannah's Plant Riverside District. A glass of wine, local beers, or signature cocktails, they are all very much worth a visit. If you need to nibble on something, try one of their signature desserts, which rotate on their menu seasonally.

THE RIVER STREET CRAWL

1. **DUB'S PUB,** 225 W. RIVER ST., SAVANNAH, (912) 200-3652, DUBSRIVERSTREET.COM

2. **OLYMPIA CAFE,** 5 E. RIVER ST., SAVANNAH, (912) 233-3131, OLYMPIACAFE.NET

3. **THE WAREHOUSE BAR & GRILLE,** 18 E. RIVER ST., SAVANNAH, (912) 234-6003, THEWAREHOUSEBARANDGRILLE.COM

4. **HUEY'S ON THE RIVER,** 115 E. RIVER ST., SAVANNAH, (912) 234-7385, HUEYSONTHERIVER.NET

5. **THE COTTON EXCHANGE TAVERN,** 201 E. RIVER ST., SAVANNAH, (912) 232-7088, SITES.GOOGLE.COM/VIEW/THE-COTTON-EXCHANGE-TAVERN

6. **SAVANNAH'S CANDY KITCHEN,** 225 E. RIVER ST., SAVANNAH, (912) 233-8411, SAVANNAHCANDY.COM

7. **BOAR'S HEAD GRILL & TAVERN,** 1 LINCOLN STREET RAMP, SAVANNAH, (912) 651-9660, BOARSHEADGRILLANDTAVERN.COM

8. **RIVER STREET LIQUOR,** 425 E. RIVER ST., SAVANNAH, (912) 944-4449, RIVERSTREETLIQUOR.COM

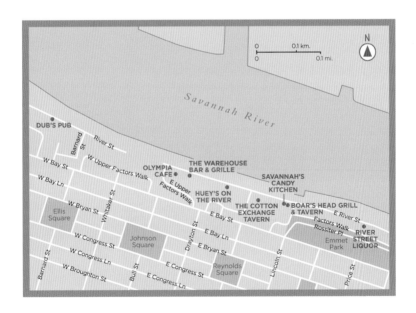

River Street

The Original

For decades, the first things anyone would mention after "Savannah, Georgia" were two more words: "River Street." Savannah has grown enough to where that isn't nearly the case anymore, but River Street remains one of our city's main attractions. And for very good reason.

If you are visiting Savannah, you must have, to some extent anyway, an interest in history. Well, River Street is our front row to all of that history, almost literally. After all, it was on the riverfront in 1733 near what is now city hall that General James Oglethorpe first landed in Savannah with an almost immediate plan to settle here and begin a colony. By the middle 1800s, Savannah was the leading exporter of cotton in the world. That meant lots of commerce on the waterfront. Ships arrived filled with ballast stone for balance. The stones were emptied and later used to create the cobblestone streets you see today. The ships would then leave full of cotton and other exports. That included slaves, who were temporarily housed in a lot of the buildings you see along the waterfront today.

Speaking of today, River Street remains a picture-perfect postcard of what Savannah is to this day. Taverns, restaurants, and shops dot the scene along River Street. They offer visitors a unique opportunity to step inside while at the same time stepping back in time to see as much original architectural detail as you will in any historic city.

1

DUB'S PUB

We chose to begin this crawl on the western end of River Street because it lies in the shadow of our first stop, the Plant Riverside District. The bars and shops you see on this end of River Street are, in the big picture, new to the scene. That is, except for **DUB'S PUB**.

Dub's Pub serves a lot of purposes on West River Street. The food is good, the bar is well stocked, and there are a ton of televisions all over the restaurant. It is why they bill themselves as River Street's "only sports pub." They are probably right. On Saturdays in the fall, Dub's will fill with college football fans looking to catch their favorite team. That would include locals making their way down to River Street to watch their Georgia Bulldogs.

The jalapeño beer cheese dip, topped with pico de gallo and cilantro and served with soft pretzel bites, is a standard fare go-to at Dub's. I've enjoyed it many times. My favorite, though, is their Dub's Burger. I'm not sure if it is their most popular, but it very well could be. Burger topped and dripping with that jalapeño beer cheese we just mentioned, bacon, and spicy ketchup (which I get on the side to keep the mess to a minimum).

Dub's offers a generous selection of local beers on tap as well as regional brews. The standout beverage here, though, could be their pepper-infused vodka Bloody Mary. Take a walk up to the bar and see it for yourself. Some like it hot. If that's you, then this one is for you.

Savannah's St. Patrick's Day celebration is Savannah's biggest festival of the year and widely believed to be a top five largest in America. A lot of the celebration following the parade takes place here on River Street. Unlike Chicago, we do not turn our river green.

---

2 OLYMPIA CAFE

OLYMPIA CAFE has been a centerpiece on Savannah's River Street for over 30 years, so they must be doing something right. Located at the foot of the Drayton Street ramp in the shadow of Savannah City Hall, Olympia remains Savannah's only "Greek taverna" in the spirit of those you will find anywhere you travel in Greece. This is why it very well could be Savannah's most popular River Street restaurant for locals who generally resist traveling down to more visitor-centric sections of Savannah. We most certainly do, but we pick our spots meticulously. Olympia is one of them.

If you stop in at Olympia, you can eat a lot or a little bit. On the menu, keeping it simple is the gyro, slices of gyro meat in a warm pita with cool house-made tzatziki. During a recent "gyro tour of Savannah," we decided that if this wasn't Savannah's best, it was definitely in the top two. Yes, it is that good.

Olympia offers a full menu of salads, seafood, and steaks, all served with traditional Greek accompaniments. The moussaka (baked eggplant) and spanakopita (spinach cheese pie) are classic Greek dishes that remain popular here as well.

Keep in mind that Olympia Cafe is a sit-down restaurant. They have an adjacent ice cream shop that serves some of their more "fast food"–type items with some sidewalk seating if you'd like to grab a snack to enjoy on the waterfront.

> The 1996 Olympic Games were held in Atlanta, 4 hours away by car. Olympic yachting events were held here in Savannah due to its proximity to the ocean, a few miles away.

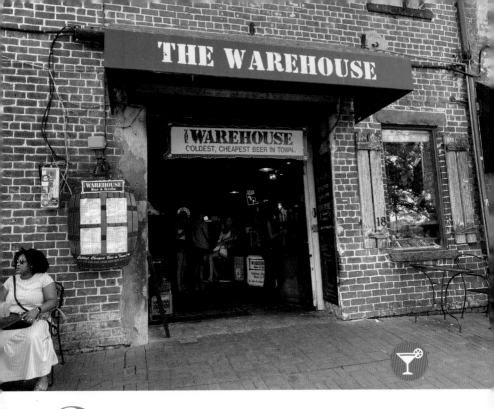

3

THE WAREHOUSE BAR & GRILLE

THE WAREHOUSE on River Street proudly claims to possess the "coldest, cheapest beer in town." While I don't know if that is necessarily true, I can say that they have perhaps the largest—and most convenient—selection of draft beers on this end of River Street. Especially when you consider the taps begin about 4 feet inside of their double-wide doorway. Grab-and-go brews? Absolutely. Remember, you can walk with your beverages in Savannah.

If you want to take a load off your feet and cool off, step inside. They have several tables and televisions for the game-watching crowd and a full menu of burgers, wings, and other fried bar food goodies. My go-to here is the chicken wings, served in 5-, 10-, or 15-piece portions in close to 2 dozen different flavors. I love the traditional hot. Just enough lip smackin' heat and tang to keep me happy.

In the big picture, the space is small and cavernous. That's what you get with these old buildings. There's a pool table toward the back for those who want to enjoy while watching a ball game on television. Just keep in mind, if you stay in the Warehouse too long, you will leave here smelling like a fried chicken wing. Not that there is anything wrong with that. The food is good, but more times than not this is my hit-and-run refill spot on the way down River Street.

4

HUEY'S ON THE RIVER

I have many times referred to Savannah as "the Little Easy" as an homage to one of my favorite cities in America. Of course, that's the Big Easy, New Orleans. There are definite similarities between the two when you consider their histories, architecture, and overall lifestyle, but the gap is significant when you compare cuisines between the two. That is nothing to be ashamed of; really, how many American cities can put their food up against the best of New Orleans? Not too many. All of that said, **HUEY'S ON THE RIVER** is Savannah's only true taste of New Orleans.

Serving classic Cajun and Creole dishes, Huey's is different from a lot of the eateries along River Street because their entire restaurant front is glass, which offers a wide view of the Savannah River and people watching along River Street.

The gumbo is tasty, as are the red beans and rice. Probably the star of the show here at Huey's is their Sunday brunch featuring a wide variety of Benedicts. I'm a big fan of the crab cake Benedict, served on a toasted

English muffin and topped with a fried green tomato, but the fried chicken Benedict is always turning heads. Huey's also serves Savannah's best beignets, no question. They are served on a huge plate under a mountain of powdered sugar. They are delicious and a draw for locals unto themselves.

As is their Bloody Mary, which at one point was considered the best in town. Whether it still holds that title today is subjective, but it remains an exceptional version of that classic cocktail. Don't have time to hang around? Grab one to go and enjoy it as you make your way through the rest of your crawl.

5 THE COTTON EXCHANGE TAVERN

Did someone mention Bloody Marys? If the Bloody at Huey's isn't River Street's best, then the one at **THE COTTON EXCHANGE TAVERN** very much is. This tavern is a River Street institution and everything you would expect to find in a hundreds-of-years-old waterfront venue. Dominated by dark woods, rock walls, and absolutely zero pretense, the Cotton Exchange is the kind of place that converts tourists into regulars. More than once I've had visitors tell me their very first stop during a visit to Savannah is the Cotton Exchange. Yes, even before they've checked into their hotel room.

So what's the draw? For starters, those Bloody Marys we mentioned are absolutely among the best in town. Any local who is truly in the know will tell you that. Their Bloody Mary mix is made in-house every single day and it tastes like it. Beyond that, the Tybee Crab Chowder is a huge draw here. Crabmeat, corn, and potato in a creamy chowder with just a tiny bit of spice for a kick. It is regularly their top-selling item on the menu and it is an appetizer, so that will give you an idea of how much people love it.

Spanky's on River Street is a local dining institution. It is where they say they invented the chicken finger in 1976. There is no record of anything similar in America before that time.

6

SAVANNAH'S CANDY KITCHEN

In the mid '70s, the Strickland family opened a furniture store on Savannah's riverfront. As you might imagine, business wasn't great. People weren't necessarily coming down to the waterfront to buy a chair or a desk. Somewhere along the line, they decided to purchase a used soft-serve ice cream machine as a way to entice customers to come in and take a look. Not only did it work, but they've created an empire around it.

Using recipes handed down from generation to generation, SAVANNAH'S CANDY KITCHEN and their sister property River Street Sweets have become a national brand with locations from Key West to San Antonio to Utah. But it all started here on River Street in Savannah.

There's a good chance you will smell it before you see it. Those are the Southern pecan pralines that are made in-house every day. Of course, not everything they sell nationally is made here, but they do still make quite a bit from scratch right before your eyes.

In addition to the pralines, there's the fudge, ice cream, and taffy. All of it made in-house. It doesn't matter how old you are, if you walk in here, you become a kid in a candy store that oozes nostalgia from every 200-plus-year-old brick in the walls.

The candy apples in several different flavors are always a big hit, but if you are looking to grab something to toss in your bag for a late-night nosh in your hotel room, it's hard to pass on the pecan turtles or a delicious piece of peanut butter fudge. Just remember, it can get hot and humid around here. You'll have to be mindful of the temperature unless you want to pull a melted string of chocolatey goo out of your bag or purse later.

Don't want to carry all this sweet goodness around? Savannah's Candy Kitchen will ship worldwide to your front door. You can order it here, or wait until you get home and do it all online. That will save you the awkward looks you'll get at the airport when you screen that duffle full of 45 pounds of sweets.

Also note, we've listed Savannah's Candy Kitchen in this crawl, but there is also a River Street Sweets location on River Street. Yes, it can get confusing if you are not familiar, but they generally offer the same goodies under the same umbrella. Just two different storefronts and still family owned and operated.

7 BOAR'S HEAD GRILL & TAVERN

If you are looking for a place to enjoy a wonderful sit-down dinner on historic River Street, then **BOAR'S HEAD GRILL & TAVERN** should be on your very short list for consideration. Much like the rest of River Street, this building was a former warehouse. This particular section was built in 1780.

The Boar's Head restaurant has been in this spot since 1959. In 1998 it was renovated to what you see today. Views of the river and passing cargo ships are largely limited to window seats, but if you can get one (something you will likely need a reservation for), then the scene becomes a snapshot trapped in time and a top reason why so many people visit Savannah in the first place.

Their she-crab soup deserves a mention here. If you aren't familiar with she-crab soup, it's a very rich, thick soup made with heavy cream, crab or fish stock, and crabmeat, of course. Traditionally, crab roe and a tiny amount of sherry are added. It's a staple on menus up the road in Charleston, but you can find it hither and yon in Savannah. Including here at Boar's Head.

8 RIVER STREET LIQUOR

RIVER STREET LIQUOR remains one of Savannah's best-kept secrets on the waterfront. If, of course, your crawls call for something more than soft drinks. We've already established the fact that you are free to roam about the city carrying anything you care to drink, but River Street Liquor sells beer—and more, of course—at a fraction of the price you will find in any restaurant or bar along the river.

Just looking for a quick beer? You can either grab one to go at a restaurant's bar, or you can walk in here, grab a single out of the cooler, and pay less than half the price. They'll even give you a souvenir cup for your trouble.

The same goes for bottles of any spirit you may want to take back to your room. No, you are not allowed to walk down the street drinking from a glass handle of vodka, but you are absolutely allowed to pour yourself a drink and sippity doo-dah your way across town. Just put the original containers away, behave yourself, and enjoy responsibly. No one is going to bug you. This applies to any liquor store you will encounter in downtown Savannah.

BAY STREET AND
THE EASTERN WHARF PROJECT CRAWL

1. **CHURCHILL'S,** 13 W. BAY ST., SAVANNAH, (912) 232-8501, CHURCHILLSONBAY.COM

2. **MOON RIVER BREWING COMPANY,** 21 W. BAY ST., SAVANNAH, (912) 447-0943, MOONRIVERBREWING.COM

3. **VIC'S ON THE RIVER,** 26 E. BAY ST., SAVANNAH, (912) 721-1000, VICSONTHERIVER.COM

4. **TREYLOR PARK,** 115 E. BAY ST., SAVANNAH, (888) 873-9567, TREYLORPARK.COM

5. **CAFE M,** 128 E. BAY ST., SAVANNAH, (912) 712-3342, CAFEMSAVANNAH.COM

6. **208 WINE BAR,** 208 E. BAY ST., SAVANNAH, (912) 777-4240, 208WINEBAR.COM

7. **B. MATTHEW'S EATERY,** 325 E. BAY ST., SAVANNAH, (912) 233-1319, BMATTHEWSEATERY.COM

8. **FLEETING (EASTERN WHARF PROJECT),** 201 PORT ST., SAVANNAH, (912) 521-6150, FLEETINGRESTAURANT.COM

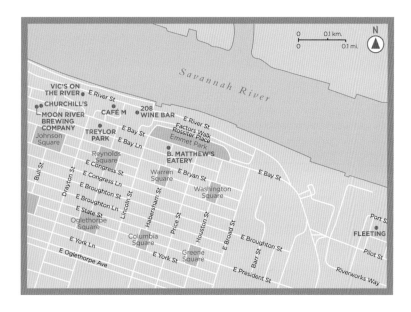

Bay Street and The Eastern Wharf Project

"We Don't Really Want to Go All the Way to the River"

Bay Street is downtown Savannah's first—and busiest—thoroughfare once you make your way up the bluff from River Street. Along Bay, you will find a similar set of choices to what you will encounter on the river, but you'll find them on both sides of the street because you are not bordered by water on one side.

This is your introduction to the true charm of Savannah. Live oak trees dripping with Spanish moss line the street, offering a welcome respite from the strength of the sun.

Quite obviously, these buildings are all historic as well and protected as such. Bay Street is home not only to Savannah City Hall (built in 1905) and the US Customs House (built in 1852) but also a significant variety of hotels, restaurants, bars, and shops. On this crawl you will likely see three or four times as many potential places to pop in on, as we will mention on the crawl. When you include the two riverview rooftops that are accessible from Bay Street, you could probably spend half a day making your way down Bay Street, but we are here to offer some highlights. You can find those rooftop venues in our rooftop appendix.

Bay Street is also where you will find Factors Walk, a nearly half-mile-long alleyway between Bay and River Streets that once served as a roadway for delivery wagons arriving at or departing from the waterfront. Pedestrian gangways, many of which are still in place, allowed merchants to inspect the cargo from above.

1

CHURCHILL'S

CHURCHILL'S is one of Savannah's more popular pubs, certainly the largest. Featuring a healthy selection of beers on tap, including local brews, Churchill's is the one spot on Bay Street where you are likely to find a member of the food and beverage industry enjoying a pint after work.

The food is good. Try the scotch egg or the steak and ale pie, made with onions and mushrooms and topped with a homemade flaky pastry. The real reason to stop here is for a beverage, either indoors at their massive main bar, or upstairs on their second-floor patio, which looks out onto Johnson Square behind the building. Some will try to qualify this as a "Savannah rooftop." It is not. For starters, rooftops are on the roof. This is a lovely outdoor setting on the smallish side with a bar of its own to enjoy, but it is underqualified as a rooftop bar. Though it is very enjoyable when the weather cooperates.

2 MOON RIVER BREWING COMPANY

Long before Savannah had a "local beer scene," it had the **MOON RIVER BREWING COMPANY,** housed in a building widely considered to be among the most haunted in the city. Built in 1821 as the City Hotel (Savannah's first hotel), it also served as a post office and a branch of the Bank of the United States. The last guest checked out of the City Hotel in 1864, just before Savannah returned to the control of the United States Army in the Civil War.

I beg to present you as a Christmas gift the City of Savannah.
—William Tecumseh Sherman, December 1864
in a telegram to President Lincoln

In 1999, Moon River debuted in its current state as a brew pub. As we mentioned, widespread local beers were still about a decade away, so Moon River developed a large following with locals and visitors looking for a unique pour. The beer garden you see at the corner of Bay and Drayton Streets was added later as a further indicator of this location's popularity.

Moon River offers about a dozen brews, all made on the premises, There are some regulars like the Yoga Pants and the Swamp Fox (IPA), plus some on a rotation.

The food offers a little bit of something for everyone. Standard pub fare. Chicken wings, burgers, and sandwiches as well as a number of entrée-sized selections. Much like Churchill's before it, grab a nosh if you'd like, but what makes Moon River different are the beers and the vibe. The food will get a little more interesting as we move along in our crawl.

TIP

Savannah City Hall offers free guided tours of the building on the first Tuesday of every month at noon. The tours are limited in space and advance registration is required. Find more information at savannahga.gov.

3

VIC'S ON THE RIVER

Exiting Moon River, with Savannah City Hall directly in front, you will continue east (to the right) and across Bay Street. Just to the east of city hall you will find "Washington's Guns," a set of Revolutionary War cannons that George Washington captured at the Battle of Yorktown. He gifted the cannons to Savannah following a visit in 1791.

Just beyond those cannons as you look north toward the river is a Savannah classic restaurant, **VIC'S ON THE RIVER**.

You won't find too many fine dining restaurants on our crawls, but if we had to mention a select few, Vic's on the River would be on that short list.

While a proper dinner at Vic's can be sensational, stopping in for a bite to eat or lunch at their bar should not be overlooked. The room is beautiful with several large windows offering views of the waterfront. Later in the afternoon, their signature grand piano comes alive in the bar area, offering a great setting for a midafternoon glass of wine and a couple of appetizers.

Speaking of that food, the fried green tomatoes are a calling card here, as are the shrimp and grits and the crab cake. If you'd like to go a little heavier on the indulgence, the pecan fried flounder is a Savannah signature dish that you will find at a select few eateries around town but nowhere else. At Vic's it is served with an Andouille sausage and potato hash and citrus honey butter.

You get the idea; this is serious Southern eating inspired by the flavors of the Georgia coast. It's not for everyone, but it is certainly worth a peek if this is more your speed.

4 TREYLOR PARK

Back across Bay Street and 1 block or so to the east, you will be about as far away from the elegance and charm of Vic's on the River as you can get when you arrive at one of the most popular eateries in Savannah, TREYLOR PARK.

The name is a play on words from one of its owners, Trey Wilder. Trey moved to Savannah nearly a decade ago with a vision to open a restaurant that offered comfort food, yes, but something different than you'd find anywhere else. The kinds of foods, he said at the time, that could be popular . . . in a trailer park. They've succeeded.

Within two years of Treylor Park opening, they were mentioned in the *New York Times* as a place to visit if you had 36 hours in Savannah. The rest, as they like to say, is history. Treylor Park on Bay Street was the first of now three locations they operate in downtown Savannah. Liberty Street's Treylor Park–Hitch is one; Treylor Park's Double Wide Diner (also on Bay Street) is the other. They also have one other location outside of Jacksonville, Florida.

The menu got Savannah's attention almost immediately by offering off-the-wall spins on the most common items. The PB&J chicken wings sound almost too ridiculous

The Savannah Cotton Exchange at 100 East Bay Street was built in 1876. Its primary purpose was to set the market price for cotton exports to New York or London. It closed in 1951. It has served as Solomon's Masonic Lodge since 1976.

to believe, until you actually bite into one and think you are eating a fried peanut butter and jelly sandwich.

The menu has grown quite a bit since day one, but the chicken and pancake tacos are a day-one classic. Your taco shells are not shells at all, but small pancakes that wrap around your serving of fried chicken, chili aioli, and strawberry salsa. Intrigued yet?

Maybe my favorite in the building (and that's saying something) is another Treylor Park original. Treylor Park Nachos Grande. There are no chips in sight. Your platter comes piled high with waffle fries topped with diced fried chicken chunks, bacon, cheddar cheese, chive ranch, and a balsamic gastrique. This particular dish is absolutely big enough to share, but I know plenty of people who have taken it down themselves. It's legendary around here.

Their original Bay Street location has a tiny beer garden out back, complete with a six-seat bar offering several local and regional beers on tap plus a doorway out into the lane behind it in the event you just want to slip out the back door.

Treylor Park also offers a very popular brunch service at their three Savannah locations should you find yourself drawn back to their over-the-top goodness.

5 CAFE M

Directly across Bay Street from the insanity that can be a visit to Treylor Park is perhaps Bay Street's most peaceful hideaway. **CAFE M** French cafe.

Cafe M was created by a French couple who, like so many others, visited Savannah and fell in love with the city. Their vision was to offer classic French pastries, coffees, and salads along Factors Walk and in the shadow of Savannah City Hall's golden dome. The spot was almost an instant hit not only with visitors but also locals who work in the area looking for a healthier option for lunch. One step inside and you are immediately transported to a Parisian cafe. If the smell of freshly baked bread doesn't get you, well then, the chocolate croissant almost certainly will.

The Provence on a freshly baked baguette is our first of many wonderful choices. Prosciutto, mozzarella, sun-dried tomatoes, and mixed greens are tough to beat in my book. We've also very much enjoyed the Normandy, which features brie, pears, ham, walnuts, and dried cranberries.

Beyond the sandwiches, salads, and quiches, Cafe M also offers brunch service with a selection of mimosas and wine. It is worthy of a mention here that Cafe M is a morning or early afternoon type of visit. They generally close for the day in the middle of the afternoon.

6

208 WINE BAR

Keeping on the "river side" of Bay Street and just a few steps across the pedestrian bridge that crosses the Abercorn Street access ramp to River Street is the antithesis of the early in the day joys of Cafe M. As you make your way to 208 East Bay Street, you will first notice Two Cracked Eggs Cafe. Two Cracked Eggs is not getting its own entry on our crawl, but you should

keep it in mind for breakfast. Their biscuits are made in-house, huge and as fluffy as your favorite pillow. Please make a note of it.

Instead, on this crawl, we continue another hundred or so feet to one of the few true wine bars in Savannah. It is certainly the only one on Bay Street.

208 WINE BAR is relatively new to the Savannah scene, but it was an instant hit. It was created by James Divine and Christina Pirovits to fill a void in the market. There is no shortage of places you can grab a beer or something stronger along Bay Street but nowhere to quietly enjoy a glass of wine with good conversation and picture-perfect views of the Savannah River.

The bar is large and inviting. The selection of wines, both new world and old world, is creative with a lean away from the usual suspects. Nine times out of 10, one or both of the owners are behind the bar offering a depth of knowledge about anything they are pouring.

There is no regular offering of food at 208, but they do hold regular tastings and events that include some local nibbles you can enjoy during a wine tasting. You can find a calendar of events on their website.

7 B. MATTHEW'S EATERY

Exiting 208 Wine Bar and to the left, continue several hundred feet to one of the few public parks in downtown Savannah. In this case, Emmett Park. It is more of a green space than an actual park, but it is where you will find Savannah's Vietnam War Monument and our Celtic Cross. The latter dedicated to all Savannah citizens of Irish descent.

Directly in front of Emmett Park and back across Bay Street you will find **B. MATTHEW'S EATERY** at the corner of Bay and Habersham Streets.

B. Matthew's began as a neighborhood deli and bakery in 2002. Later, it evolved into a full-service eatery but still largely dedicated to the neighborhood tucked behind it. At the time, it was one of the few places in the entire city you could find a proper brunch

About a decade or so ago, B. Matthew's was named Best Breakfast in the State of Georgia. A well-deserved honor and a distinction that moved this neighborhood joint front and center before any visitor to our city.

The history in this building is rich, dating back to the 1700s. The title deed refers to it as "the oldest tavern in the South," which is fascinating when you consider how far back Savannah's settlement goes (1733).

The space has been renovated many times. Today it maintains a truly historical feel but with modern accents. It remains one of Savannah's most popular brunch spots (reservations recommended). The Bay Street Scramble may be their most popular: eggs, bacon, tomato, green onions, and cheese topped with a delicious mornay sauce.

The shrimp and grits at B. Matthew's have always been delicious: shrimp, tasso ham, and heirloom tomatoes with a white wine cream sauce topped with collard greens and green onions. They are a brunch staple but also available for dinner. That's how it goes in Savannah with our shrimp and grits.

8

FLEETING (EASTERN WHARF PROJECT)

Worthy of a mention here simply because it is one of Savannah's top two or three restaurants. Located a solid half mile down Bay Street and beyond the Riverfront Marriott Hotel is the still very new Eastern Wharf project, anchored by the very trendy Thompson Hotel. Its rooftop (13 stories up) is called Bar Julian. It offers Savannah's best sunsets to go along with great food and drink.

The ground-floor restaurant at the Thompson is called FLEETING and it is sensational. The list of kitchens in Savannah that use local ingredients this well is very short. With dishes like koji aged duck breast served with Carolina Gold rice powder or a masa crusted red snapper with field pea salad, charred guajillo salsa, and lime, Fleeting delivers on what so many Southern restaurants promise but fall short on.

This is fine dining, yes, but not even close to Savannah's most expensive restaurant. It is worthy of a look from the foodie in your life.

It is also worth mentioning that the Thompson is just off the center of downtown Savannah. Just beyond what would be considered a comfortable walk. Unless you are staying there, transportation to and from is highly recommended.

ELLIS SQUARE AND CITY MARKET CRAWL

1. **SORRY CHARLIE'S OYSTER BAR,** 116 W. CONGRESS ST., SAVANNAH, (912) 234-5397, SORRYCHARLIES.COM

2. **B&D BURGERS CONGRESS STREET,** 209 W. CONGRESS STREET, SAVANNAH, (912) 785-1070, BDBURGERS.NET

3. **THE GROVE,** 301 W. CONGRESS ST., SAVANNAH, (912) 777-7597, THEGROVESAVANNAH.COM

4. **THE BAR AT GARIBALDI,** 315 W. CONGRESS ST., SAVANNAH, (912) 232-7118, GARIBALDISAVANNAH.COM

5. **THE RAIL PUB AND CONGRESS STREET SOCIAL CLUB,** 411 W. CONGRESS ST., SAVANNAH, (912) 238-1985, CONGRESSSTREETSOCIALCLUB.COM

6. **VINNIE VAN GOGO'S,** 317 W. BRYAN ST., SAVANNAH, (912) 233-6394, VINNIEVANGOGO.COM

7. **THE LITTLE CROWN PUB BY PIE SOCIETY,** 19 JEFFERSON ST., SAVANNAH, (912) 650-0050, THEBRITISHPIECOMPANY.COM

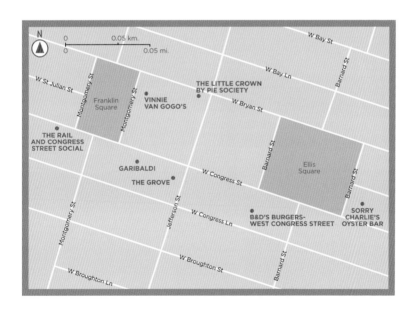

Ellis Square and City Market

Savannah's Fun Square

Shortly after his arrival in 1733, General James Oglethorpe laid out a plan for what would become Savannah in the form of a grid. A total of 24 "town squares" filled this grid. Colonists lived around each square; in some cases, livestock was kept in the center. There were also separate lots around the squares dedicated to community buildings.

Today, most of the squares are intact with an almost even split between residential and commercial surroundings. None of them, however, can compare to what you will find at Ellis Square. With City Market steps to the west, there is no question that Ellis Square is Savannah's center of recreational activity.

Ellis Square and City Market generally appeal to a younger demographic, but that doesn't at all mean that there isn't something for everyone. Boutique hotels, restaurants, rooftop hangouts, live music venues, and bars. Fine dining, street food, breakfast, lunch, dinner, and anything in between. If you can't find it in the Ellis Square / City Market section of downtown Savannah, it is unlikely you will find it anywhere.

This is, without question, the most commercially dense section of downtown Savannah. We could create five crawls to navigate it all, depending on your particular flavor of fun.

Ellis Square was also known as Marketplace Square. From the 1730s until the 1950s, it served as a center of commerce in Savannah. That also included the sale of slaves until December 1864 and the arrival of the Union army.

This one promises to have a little bit of something for everyone.

Ellis Square sits on top of one of the City of Savannah's public parking garages, which makes a visit easier. The entirety of the garage is underground, with elevators positioned at a few different spots to return you to street level and the middle of all the action.

1

SORRY CHARLIE'S OYSTER BAR

Sixteen million or so visitors make their way to Savannah, Georgia, each and every year. It's a good bet that perhaps 15 million of those arrive in town asking the same question: "Where do we go for seafood?" Hard to believe, I know, but downtown Savannah is lacking in what you would call a full-blown seafood restaurant. Sure, there are a few options on River Street, but if you're looking for anything remotely modern or even progressive, then **SORRY CHARLIE'S OYSTER BAR** is your best bet.

Towering four stories above Ellis Square at the corner of Congress and Barnard Streets, Sorry Charlie's is your most convenient spot for anything seafood. That would include a large selection of raw oysters brought in from various locations along the East Coast, served chilled on a bed of ice. Those options change daily.

In addition to the raw, you can enjoy roasted oysters in a variety of ways, plus a full menu of seafood dishes including po' boys, fish tacos, shrimp cocktail, and more. Meanwhile, the Fish House Punch, featuring peach brandy, cognac, dark rum, and lemon juice, is a crowd pleaser. It is batched in-house and available on tap.

On the third floor of this building, you will find the Bamboo Room Tiki Bar. If you are into the fruity drink thing and the Fish House Punch wasn't good enough for you, then a stop here is a must. On a hot summer day in Savannah, the cool darkness of the Tiki Bar offers a perfect escape from the elements.

There's also a rooftop bar here at Sorry Charlie's.

2

B&D BURGERS CONGRESS STREET

As you leave Sorry Charlie's with Ellis Square just ahead of you, cross over Congress Street and make your way west and away from Sorry Charlie's. On your left you will see two popular bars including Barrelhouse South and one restaurant on the corner of Congress and Barnard Street, Coco and Moss.

Crossing over Barnard and continuing up Congress, you may hear your next stop before you see it. Especially if it's college football season. Just ahead on the left you will find **B&D BURGERS**. One of their two downtown Savannah locations. What makes this one different and more appealing is the size. B&D Congress is two stories tall and features a massive outdoor area that serves as a game day gathering spot.

There are televisions throughout the inside of the restaurant as well, but fair warning. If the Georgia Bulldogs are playing, you may have a hard time getting another game on any of them. If you don't know already, you should. Football in the South is an immovable force, particularly on Saturdays between September and December. All of it is good natured, of course, but still consumed with all the seriousness and focus of a pilot trying to land a 747 on a yoga mat.

B&D is a good spot for lunch. Their selection of burgers, to include veggie, bison, chicken, or turkey burgers, is the largest in the city. You can build your own or go with one of their specialties like the Wormsloe, topped with a fried green tomato and pimento cheese, or the Fort Jackson. That burger is topped with their creamy buffalo dip and bacon. If you're not hungry for a full meal yourself, you can try some of their sliders. They come 2 to an order and are perfect for sharing with a side of their house-made fries.

If the games are on and you care to enjoy, they offer a full liquor bar and several local beers on tap. If you are out of season and are ready to roll, then your next stop awaits.

3

THE GROVE

Heading back out onto Congress Street and to the left, you will continue a block or so across Jefferson Street to the three-story white building on that corner just in front of you. The Grove.

Very popular with the younger crowd and bachelorette parties, **THE GROVE** Restaurant and Rooftop Bar bills itself as a sophisticated casual restaurant, which is true. It does offer a little bit of something for everyone. Downstairs, on the ground floor, you can enjoy a snack at the bar or dinner in one of their dining rooms. Or you can take your party to the third-floor rooftop and enjoy a beautiful view of Savannah's downtown skyline while you make your way through a scaled-down version of their menu.

Speaking of the menu, it is rather straightforward bar food. A selection of small plates, salads, sandwiches, and burgers. I've always been a fan of the chicken tenders here. Buttermilk fried and served crispy with a cool dip on the side. The Nashville hot chicken with roasted garlic mashed potatoes and crispy brussels sprouts is maybe my favorite item on the menu.

On the drink side, there is a lot to choose from here at the Grove, especially as you get into the evening. You can enjoy a Rosemary Sweet Tea, featuring vodka mixed with a rosemary-infused tea, lemonade, and honey. Or the beverage you will eventually see; it is only a matter of time. That's the Champagne Pop. Brut bubbles paired with a fruity popsicle. Yes, dropped straight into your glass of bubbly.

If none of that appeals to you and you've got a few other people with you, you can take a shot at the Grand Mule: 192 ounces (that is not a typo) of vodka, ginger beer, and fresh lime juice. You'll know it when you see it and you'll very likely see a group of young ladies hovering over one with colorful straws pointing in every direction. Welcome to the Grove.

The statue at the west end of Ellis Square before City Market is that of Hollywood songwriter and Savannah native Johnny Mercer. He was famous for writing such songs as "Moon River" and "Hooray for Hollywood." He received 19 Oscar nominations for music, winning 4. His statue was placed in this location because his descendants knew he'd prefer to be in the middle of the action in Savannah.

4 THE BAR AT GARIBALDI

With the Grove in your rear view, step back out the front door onto Congress Street and turn left. Just ahead you on the left you will see Molly MacPherson's Pub, Savannah's only Scottish pub where they claim to own the largest selection of single malt scotch on the East Coast. It certainly is in Savannah. Pop in here if you'd like or continue on to their next-door neighbor: Garibaldi Seafood Restaurant.

THE BAR AT GARIBALDI is not a separate brand nor does it possess a different identity from the rest of the restaurant. Not at all. What it is, though, is classic Savannah. Sister restaurant to the very popular the Olde Pink House, Garibaldi was a firehouse circa 1871. If you are allowed to take a peek at their upstairs dining room, you will still see the pole Savannah's firemen slid down on their way to work.

Garibaldi is also one of Savannah's best-regarded old-school restaurants. The full menu is available at the bar, and it is not at all uncommon to see it lined with locals squeezing in a happy hour sip and or nosh before heading home, or staying for a full dinner. Sometimes there's a traffic jam at the bar.

The Denver lamb ribs with a sweet ginger soy glaze and cabbage slaw get my vote for a top two to three dish in the city. It's a small portion, appetizer sized for sharing at the bar, but the full menu is available. The veal chop au poivre turns heads every single time one comes out of the kitchen.

THE RAIL PUB AND CONGRESS STREET SOCIAL CLUB

As you leave Garibaldi and turn left to continue up Congress Street, you will reach the intersection of Congress and Montgomery Streets with Franklin Square to your right.

This corner is a fork in the road that many Savannahians have faced more than once. Continue up Congress and venture deeper into the abyss or cross over Congress Street back into City Market toward something more closely resembling a leisurely stroll. For the record, I've

done both plenty of times, so I will share both with you. Beginning with one of the most popular dive bars in the state of Georgia.

Straight up Congress and immediately across Montgomery Street is "the Rail."

THE RAIL PUB is undoubtedly a Savannah institution. Depending on who you ask, it is the most popular dive bar in town. Where else will you find $1 "Ghetto Dogs," $5 40s, and free fried chicken on Friday nights? The building dates back to 1890 and gets its name for the railroad workers who would gather across the street in Franklin Square.

These days, I like to think there are two different versions of the Rail depending on the day of the week. One is a quiet, no-nonsense bar offering cold beer and a friendly bartender. The other—generally on weekends—can become a caricature of what I believe a dive bar is supposed to be. Long lines, beer tubs, and outrageous crowds aren't my idea of dive bar utopia (not to say I've not been there during both). It's big enough and there is plenty of room for everyone. Just don't puke on me, y'all.

Two doors down you will find the CONGRESS STREET SOCIAL CLUB. Very popular with the late crowd and featuring live music as well as $6 cheeseburgers, "Social" sports quite possibly the largest selection of bourbons in Savannah, no joke.

6 VINNIE VAN GOGO'S

If you choose to sidestep the Rail and or Congress Street Social and cross Congress Street itself toward City Market, you begin to make the turn and make your way back to where you started at Ellis Square.

Dating back to the 1700s, Savannah's City Market served as the city's grocery hub and the place to find other goods, too. Today it is dominated largely by art galleries, restaurants, and bars for 2 blocks until you reach Ellis Square.

At the top of the market and directly in front of you as you approach from Congress Street at Franklin Square is **VINNIE VAN GOGO'S** Pizza, another Savannah institution serving New York–style pizzas since 1991.

Largely set up with outdoor seating (there are a few tables as well as a small bar inside), "Vinnie's" is about as straightforward, no-frills as they come. Your menu, brought to you by a server, is printed on a sheet of paper. Two sizes of pies: medium or large. Pick your toppings and keep it moving. There are also spinach salads and calzones that are

> The First African Baptist Church across Franklin Square from **Vinnie Van GoGo's** pizzeria was the first African American church in North America, established in 1773. It was used as a stop along the Underground Railroad.

absolutely big enough to feed two people. You will also find a solid selection of local beers. Here's your pro tip: on Fridays and Saturdays they open for lunch, making it the perfect time to grab a slice and enjoy it on a bench in the middle of City Market.

Where else in Savannah are you going to enjoy lunch for roughly $4 plus a beverage? Good luck. Oh, and free dessert directly next door if you walk into River Street Sweets and ask for a sample of their fresh-made pralines. Go ahead, ask for two; you'll probably get them.

7 THE LITTLE CROWN PUB BY PIE SOCIETY

If you continue through City Market back toward Ellis Square, you will come upon a street you need to cross: Jefferson Street. This is not a pedestrian area; this is a regular city street, so be mindful of traffic as you make your way around. Before you cross as you face Ellis Square in the distance, look to your left. About 30 paces ahead on your left you will see Little Crown Pub on the corner of Jefferson and Bryan Streets.

LITTLE CROWN PUB is both little as well as a pub. The crown comes from the fact that it is owned and operated by Savannah's Pie Society, a local business owned and operated by a British family, thus making the crown an homage to the Royal Family.

All PIE SOCIETY does is make Savannah's most popular savory pies. Classic flavors like steak and ale pies or steak and kidney are always a hit. My personal favorite over the years has been their chicken and thyme pie. All of them baked perfectly with a buttery shortcrust pastry.

Of course, we did mention this is a pub, right? You will find 3, perhaps 4, beers on tap plus a full liquor bar offering a wonderful selection of original cocktails, like the Strawberry Fields Forever: vodka (or gin), St-Germain, and fresh strawberry puree. Harry Potter fans might enjoy the Butter Beer: vodka, butterscotch schnapps, and cream soda.

BROUGHTON STREET WEST CRAWL

1. **SPUDNIK,** 416 W. BROUGHTON ST., SAVANNAH, (912) 232-1986, SPUDNIKSAVANNAH.COM

2. **LE CAFE GOURMET,** 53 MONTGOMERY ST., SAVANNAH, (912) 200-3258, LECAFEGOURMET.COM

3. **CHOCOLAT BY ADAM TURONI,** 323 W. BROUGHTON ST., SAVANNAH, (912) 335-2914, CHOCOLATAT.COM

4. **DOTTIE'S MARKET SAVANNAH,** 257 W. BROUGHTON ST., SAVANNAH, (912) 921-9337, DOTTIESMARKETSAV.COM

5. **THE ORDINARY PUB,** 217½ W. BROUGHTON ST., SAVANNAH, (912) 238-5130, THEORDINARYPUB.COM

6. **SAVANNAH BEE COMPANY,** 104 W. BROUGHTON ST., SAVANNAH, (912) 233-7873, SAVANNAHBEE.COM

7. **THE COFFEE FOX,** 102 W. BROUGHTON ST., SAVANNAH, (912) 401-0399, THECOFFEEFOX.COM

8. **FLYING MONK NOODLE BAR,** 5 W. BROUGHTON ST., SAVANNAH, (912) 232-8888, FLYWITHTHEMONK.COM

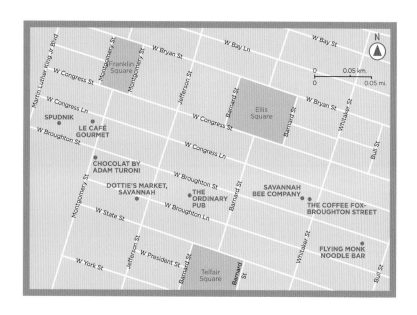

Broughton Street West

Crawling with a Lotta Bit of Shopping

Since practically the beginning of time it seems, Broughton Street has been downtown Savannah's center of commerce. Our "shopping" street. Bordered by Martin Luther King Jr. Boulevard on the west and Broad Street on the east, Broughton Street is 12 blocks long with just about two-thirds of those city blocks filled with dining and shopping options plus hotels and private residences.

Broughton Street is so dense, in fact, that we decided to split the crawls into two. The first, Broughton Street West, takes you from MLK Jr. Boulevard down to the center of Broughton at Bull Street. The Broughton Street East crawl will take you the rest of the way once you cross over Bull. There are just too many wonderful options to share, which made it that much more difficult to fit into one.

First things first: with national brands such as Urban Outfitters and H&M sprinkled among over a dozen local boutiques, you will very quickly recognize that the shopping on Broughton Street's western end ticks slightly more upscale than the choices you may encounter a few blocks up the street.

In between, of course, are several opportunities to nibble or sip along the way. Beginning with . . . the potato.

1

SPUDNIK

Leave it to Savannah to show you something you may not see anywhere else. In this case, located halfway up your first block on West Broughton Street you find what they call "the only twice baked potato restaurant in the world": Savannah's Spudnik.

When **SPUDNIK** first opened their doors, the whispers around town were consistent. How on earth was someone going to build a successful business serving nothing but baked potatoes, however creatively topped they would be? But it took off quickly and today is one of Broughton Street's more popular pit stops for students at the Savannah College of Art and Design looking for a quick and cheap bite or visitors to Savannah who just want something simple to nibble on during the day.

The variety of baked potato options is impressive. You can keep it simple with a classic potato topped with bacon, sour cream, and green onion, or you can get a little adventurous with something like the Athenian featuring roasted red pepper hummus, feta, and black olives.

There is a grilled chicken–topped potato option for carnivores and several choices for vegans. Of course, just like at any good burger joint, you can build your own potato with whatever you'd like on it. Grab one or share one. Either way you should try one. There is also a selection of soft drinks and local craft beers.

And don't forget to take a close look at the entryway. It was made by hand, entirely of pennies, ahead of Spudnik's opening.

2 LE CAFE GOURMET

As you depart Spud-nik and to the left up Broughton Street, you will pass several local shopping options. Half a block later you will reach Montgomery Street. Turn to the immediate left and you will find our next stop. Le Cafe Gourmet, one of two tastes of Paris on this crawl.

LE CAFE GOURMET is a tiny, simple French bakery and coffee shop tucked away in what is largely considered a side street between the far more active Broughton Street and City Market just ahead at Franklin Square.

Their breads, to include traditional French baguettes and more rustic round loaves, are all made in-house. As are their classic French pastries.

3 CHOCOLAT BY ADAM TURONI

Exiting Le Cafe Gourmet and making your way back toward Broughton Street, our crawl will continue to the left, across Montgomery Street. Once you cross Montgomery, cross Broughton to the southern side of the street and begin a stroll along a charming section of this street lined with excellent shopping, and one of Savannah's sweetest stops to boot. **CHOCOLAT BY ADAM TURONI**.

The shop you enter at 323 West Broughton is one of two shops that Adam and his business partner Alexandra operate in downtown Savannah. Each is unique in design and in offering exceptional bites of chocolate. Chocolate truffles, even after a decade in business, remain the gold standard for such delicacies in Savannah.

The Broughton Street location is impeccably decorated as a dining room straight out of *Alice in Wonderland*. The dining room table, a centerpiece of the room, is filled with edible goodies that you can purchase and enjoy now or perhaps later. Either way, you will love every bit of what Adam creates.

I've enjoyed so much of the goodness Adam creates over the years that it's difficult to narrow down suggestions into 1 or 2 choices. The dark chocolate peanut butter cups have been a go-to of mine for many years. As have so many of his truffles in amazingly well-developed flavors like red velvet, blood orange, or Georgia peach.

Another local favorite is the Savannah honey chocolate bar. They come 2 bars to a box each filled with what is arguably Savannah's most popular local product, Savannah Bee honey, which we will be calling on later in this crawl.

Ultimately, the choices are yours at Chocolat by Adam Turoni, and there are so many. Keep in mind that some of the truffles you will find here on Broughton Street may not be available at their Bull Street location. Of course, there is crossover, but some truffles are unique to each location. If you are unsure whether to buy some now or later, ask an employee. They will be happy to let you know what you can find where.

Shopping is my cardio.—Carrie Bradshaw, *Sex and the City*

DOTTIE'S MARKET SAVANNAH

Continuing up Broughton Street with the aforementioned shops on both sides of the street, you approach Vineyard Vines at the corner of Broughton and Jefferson. Continue across Jefferson and walk half a block. On your right you will find a Broughton Street treasure: **DOTTIE'S MARKET**.

The space is beautiful. It's a throwback to the lunch counters you found across the South in the middle of the last century. Surrounding the space is their "market," essentially a convenience store featuring anything you care to take with you to eat or drink, including sandwiches, desserts, soft drinks, bottles of wine, a single beer, and more. There is also some retail where you might find a cookbook, a picnic basket, or anything else to make your visit to Savannah a little more enjoyable.

Of course, the main draw is the food. Lunch here is among the top two or three in all of downtown Savannah. Dinner service (by reservation only) is exceptional as well. The menu can and will rotate a bit, but the roasted chicken club featuring thick-cut bacon and avocado was a show-stopper for me.

Chef Christopher Meenan is a fine-dining chef with a New York City background who, along with his wife, has created a comfortable haven with delicious food and some of the largest smiles you will find in the city.

"Dottie" is Meenan's great-grandmother, who he says "never met a stranger" and was a wonderful cook. Clearly that skill traveled well because the offerings here are outstanding.

George Washington visited Savannah and Broughton Street over 3 days in May 1791. He was greeted as a hero after the Revolutionary War. It was his only visit to the state of Georgia.

5

THE ORDINARY PUB

Walking back up toward Broughton Street, at the corner you will cross over Jefferson Street. You may notice the energy level beginning to pick up a little bit along Broughton. The very popular City Market parallels Broughton a block and a half over, so you are very likely to encounter more crowded sidewalks in this area. New York City it is not, of course, but you are, after all, approaching Savannah's center.

Halfway up the block on the right is one of three basement restaurants in the entire city. Hard to believe when you consider how old all of these buildings are. The single doorway entrance is incredibly deceiving when you make your way down the stairs and see just how big this basement space is.

THE ORDINARY PUB sits in the basement of Savannah's original Sears and Roebuck building. The owner's vision—after working in Savannah's Food and Beverage industry for years—was to create something that was neither fast food nor pretentious fine dining. He wanted a restaurant to exist right in the middle.

If you chose to eat something at our previous stop, the Grey Market, then this is your chance to cool off in a Savannah basement and enjoy a beverage or two. The food here is good, so if you are looking for that bite, the pork belly donut sliders are the way to go: 3 sliders made with dough-nuts from Savannah's most popular doughnut maker with slow-cooked pork belly and a bacon onion jam. Anytime these are in front of me, it's almost impossible to resist them. They are that delicious.

On the cocktail side, try the Bacon Old Fashioned made with bacon fat–washed bourbon, demerara, and Angostura bitters. During happy hour, you'll find most of their craft cocktails come in at under $10; that's hard to find anywhere these days, much less in the heart of Savannah.

6

SAVANNAH BEE COMPANY

We are going to give you a break from all the eating and drinking we've been doing to this point at our next stop. Once you make it to the top of the steps from the Ordinary Pub back onto Broughton Street, turn to the right and continue up Broughton Street. Your next corner is Barnard Street. The landmark is the Gap clothing store, which you will now see diagonally across Barnard. You are headed to that corner. What shape of L you use to cross is up to you.

Once you've made it diagonally across both Broughton and Barnard Streets, make your way up Broughton to the middle of the block and our next stop, the Savannah Bee Company.

SAVANNAH BEE COMPANY, like Savannah's Candy Kitchen and the Byrd Cookie Company, is a massive national brand name that got its start right here in Savannah. Founder Ted Dennard started it all as a hobby in 1999. Three years later he was running a business. Today, Savannah Bee has retail locations all across America, including two in Savannah: this one on Broughton Street and another on River Street.

If you love honey, the Broughton Street shop, like all the others, offers an opportunity to sample various honeys and—more importantly—ask questions about what you are tasting. There are specialty honeys, raw honey, and sampler gift boxes to take with you.

Also at this location is a selection of meads—an alcoholic beverage made with fermented honey—available for sampling as well.

7 THE COFFEE FOX

The good news is our next stop is short on directions because it is impossible to not find if you are at the Savannah Bee Company. **THE COFFEE FOX** is literally right next door at the corner of Broughton and Whitaker Streets.

The Coffee Fox is a member of Savannah's first family of coffee shops to include the original Foxy Loxy, Henny Penny, and their plant-based restaurant, Fox and Fig.

The Coffee Fox is one of two local coffee shops on Broughton Street; we do also have a national brand, but you can find that anywhere.

The Coffee Fox is perfect in that it offers indoor seating while you enjoy your favorite latte or cold brew. There is also a small selection of snacks to enjoy, as well as beer and wine. The affogato is a fan favorite here. Two shots of espresso poured over a scoop of ice cream.

If you can't grab a seat for some reason, you may want to consider taking a peek across the street at the Paris Market while you enjoy that beverage. The Paris Market is one of Savannah's most stunning shopping venues that also features some coffees and pastries, but the setting is a store, not just a coffee shop.

> A historical marker at Broughton and Whitaker Streets (the Coffee Fox) marks the site of Tondee's Tavern. A colonial-era gathering place for the Sons of Liberty, a clandestine organization created to fight for the rights of colonists pre-1776.

8 FLYING MONK NOODLE BAR

Now that we are sufficiently caffeinated for our stretch run, from the Coffee Fox we can cross over Whitaker Street and then back across Broughton to the southeast corner of the intersection. If you look up Whitaker Street you will see Tequila's Town, Savannah's most popular Mexican restaurant. We discuss it in more detail on our Whitaker Street crawl.

This crawl continues up Broughton Street where the next intersection is Bull Street and the center of downtown. Just before you get there, though, you will see outdoor seating and a beautiful deep red storefront. That belongs to Savannah's most popular noodle bar, **FLYING MONK**.

Flying Monk is owned by the Tran family, owners of several other restaurants in Savannah to include Madame Butterfly Korean BBQ, Coco and Moss, Flock to the Wok, Peacock Lounge, and Chive Sea Bar & Lounge—which is excellent and located directly across Broughton Street from where you are standing in front of Flying Monk.

A stop here at Flying Monk could make for excellent people watching if you choose an outside seat. Everything I've ever eaten here has been wonderful. Ramen, soups, rice dishes, all of it. If I had to pick a favorite, it would probably be the spicy lemongrass, served cold with either beef or shrimp, rice noodles, chili lime sauce, peanuts, lettuce, cucumbers, scallions, cilantro, and bean sprouts. Sound delicious?

BROUGHTON STREET EAST CRAWL

1. **KAYAK KAFE,** 1 E. BROUGHTON ST., SAVANNAH, (912) 233-6044, EATKAYAK.COM

2. **SAVANNAH SEAFOOD SHACK,** 116 E. BROUGHTON ST., SAVANNAH, (912) 344-4393, SAVANNAHSEAFOODSHACK.COM

3. **45 BISTRO,** 123 E. BROUGHTON ST, (INSIDE THE MARSHALL HOUSE HOTEL), SAVANNAH, (912) 234-1111, 45BISTRO.COM

4. **THE OLDE PINK HOUSE,** 23 ABERCORN ST., SAVANNAH, (912) 232-4286, THEOLDEPINKHOUSERESTAURANT.COM

5. **LEOPOLD'S ICE CREAM,** 212 E. BROUGHTON ST., SAVANNAH, (912) 234-4442 LEOPOLDSICECREAM.COM

6. **JAVA BURRITO COMPANY,** 420 E. BROUGHTON ST., SAVANNAH, (912) 298-5282, JAVABURRITO.COM

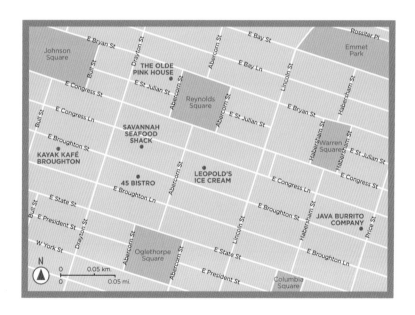

Broughton Street East

"We Hope You Saved Room for Dessert"

As we mentioned at the top of our Broughton Street West crawl, this street is far too dense for just one crawl. Too many great spots would have been left off the list. That said, there is a significant difference between the two ends of Savannah's main shopping street. The western side offers far more trendy shopping, a couple of pharmacies, and even some fast food.

At a glance, there is more going on up on the west side. But it's here on Broughton Street's east side where you are more likely to run into your neighbor or office mate. Yes, I do believe you will find far more locals on this end of Broughton Street. We'll reveal our reasons why as we make our way through the crawl. Beginning right where our Broughton Street West crawl ended, at the intersection of Broughton and Bull Streets, in the heart of Savannah.

The John Berrien House at East Broughton and Habersham is one of Savannah's oldest buildings, dating back to 1794. It was built for John Berrien, an officer in the Revolutionary War.

1

KAYAK KAFE

I've got to admit, if there is one thing that is consistently missing on these crawls, it's a solid salad. Sure, there are a ton of places in Savannah that offer one, but there are far fewer places that are dedicated exclusively to clean eats. At least not in downtown Savannah, at any rate. Our first stop absolutely fits the bill.

Located about 50 feet up East Broughton Street just beyond the corner souvenir shop is **KAYAK KAFE**, local Savannah's touchstone for those clean eats. The Broughton Street location is one of two in the city.

The Mexican salad features chopped romaine hearts, roasted chicken, pico de gallo, black beans, sliced avocado, shredded cheese, crispy tortillas strips, and spicy ranch dressing (which I usually get on the side), or the Broughton Cobb Salad.

The SCAD-owned **Jen Library** at East Broughton and Abercorn was formerly a Levy Brothers department store. The department store was ultimately absorbed by Macy's in 1988. SCAD purchased the building in 1996 and opened the library in 1998.

Kayak features several house-made salad dressings including my favorite, chipotle Caesar, and several vegetarian dressings.

The tacos and soups are also staples here at Kayak. If the weather is right, be sure to sit outside.

2

SAVANNAH SEAFOOD SHACK

With the salad stop behind us, we continue eastbound and down Broughton Street toward the next intersection, Drayton Street. Diagonally from here, you will see the other local coffee shop on Broughton Street: Blends, a Coffee Boutique. That's the corner we are headed toward, so make your way safely across the intersection and feel free to stop in for an espresso. Tell Javier we said hello.

If you are passing on the jolt of caffeine, then we will continue on this same side of Broughton just beyond the halfway point of the block. Depending on the time of year, there is a decent chance you will see a small gathering out in front of our next stop. Yes, it is that popular. It's **SAVANNAH SEAFOOD SHACK**.

Savannah Seafood Shack is home to perhaps downtown Savannah's most popular Low Country boil, a signature dish in this part of the world that goes back decades, if not longer. The dish typically consists of whole shrimp, crab, or both, boiled in a very large pot along with sausage, potatoes, and chunks of corn cobs. The best versions of the dish produce a tasty broth in which the rest of the members of this party are served.

To eat it, you get your hands plenty dirty and stinky. Much like a crawfish boil, it's very likely to create a mess. That's half the fun.

Beyond the boil, you can have practically anything you want that comes out of the ocean, as long as you want it fried. Looking for a snack? Try one of their Shack Cones filled with fried shrimp and drizzled with their house-made remoulade.

3

45 BISTRO

As you exit Savannah Seafood Shack, there's a lot to take in from this spot before we continue on our crawl. Immediately next door you will find Common Restaurant, a sister property to West Broughton's the Ordinary Pub and worth your consideration. Directly across Broughton you will see Savannah Taphouse. A two-level sports bar perfect for game day. Then there is the Marshall House Hotel in front of you. That is where we are headed.

Once you make your way across Broughton, step into the lobby of the Marshall House. Built in 1851, the Marshall House is Savannah's oldest hotel. Its history is significant. It originally served railroad workers. Later, Union troops occupied the hotel near the end of the Civil War. It was renovated in 1946 and then again in 1998, the latter producing what you see today. You can take a look at the artifacts they found during those renovations. They are on display up on the third floor.

All that history can make you thirsty, don't you think? Well, it's a good thing you can slide into their lobby bar, which also doubles as the bar for one of the most underrated old-school restaurants in the city.

45 BISTRO doesn't make the headlines, it doesn't get "Instagrammed" or "Facebooked" as much as a lot of the other venues in Savannah do, but there are a significant number of locals who will swear by it.

The menu is straightforward classic Southern, which is what a lot of people come to Savannah in search of. There are no ingredients you can't pronounce. There are no farms listed on the menu telling you where what you are enjoying came from. There is plenty of that going on elsewhere.

Try the shrimp and grits with a glass of chardonnay or maybe the pan-seared scallops topped with bacon, sweet corn ragout, and crispy shoestring potatoes. These are the flavors of old Savannah, which some people just can't get enough of.

4 THE OLDE PINK HOUSE

History lessons in the books and back out onto Broughton Street, the crawl continues to the right past Savannah Taphouse and to the next corner, which is Abercorn Street. Make your way back across Broughton; you will see Savannah's historic Lucas Theatre ahead on your right. That venue debuted on December 26, 1921. Today it is owned by the Savannah College of Art and Design.

To the right and up Broughton Street, you see one of the most popular stops in the city, Leopold's Ice Cream. We'll be coming back to that. For now, continue northbound on Abercorn toward Reynolds Square, which you will see a few hundred feet ahead.

Once you cross Congress Street and enter the tree-covered square, you will plainly see our next stop on the crawl. THE OLDE PINK HOUSE. Dating back to 1771, the Olde Pink House might be the only restaurant in Savannah with its own Wikipedia page. The history is certainly colorful and worthy of your research, but we'll share two tidbits with you.

In 1812, the home became the first bank in Georgia, Planter's Bank, for which the basement tavern is named. The vault where money was kept at the time is now a wine cellar and available for dinner seating. The second is the fact that many people consider this entire building to be haunted.

There are a few ways to enjoy Savannah's most popular culinary destination and its classic Southern delights. It all depends on what you are looking for.

Planter's Tavern downstairs (and accessible from the sidewalk just to the left of the front door) is a dark, cavernous dining room and bar. Maybe my favorite space in the city, especially in the winter with a fireplace roaring and a piano keeping the vibe in tune.

Another is the Arches Bar, back up on street level and around the left as you face the building. There is a large bar there and several tables for indoor or outdoor seating. Very popular at lunchtime with the local crowd. Lastly, you can make a reservation (highly recommended) and just walk right in through the front door for lunch or dinner. If you ask your server, they can set you up with a postmeal tour of the home. Free of charge.

5 LEOPOLD'S ICE CREAM

As you leave the Olde Pink House, you make your way back into Reynolds Square. You'll walk through the square to the right and past the already mentioned Lucas Theatre. Once you reach the corner of Abercorn and Broughton, make a left and look straight up at where we are going to satisfy your sweet tooth: Leopold's Old Fashioned Ice Cream Parlor.

If you can't tell by the line out the door, **LEOPOLD'S ICE CREAM** is incredibly popular. It's so popular simply because it is some of the best ice cream you will ever have.

Currently owned by motion picture producer Stratton Leopold and his wife Mary, it was Stratton's father and two uncles who started this Savannah phenomenon way back in 1919. The original location (not this one on Broughton Street) was a mid-1900s lunch counter frequented by all Savannahians, including Hollywood songwriting legend Johnny Mercer, who grew up in a home a couple of blocks away from the original Leopold's.

Once inside Leopold's, you find yourself surrounded by a space equal parts "old-time soda fountain" and "Hollywood movie museum." As we mentioned, Stratton is a major motion picture film producer, a profession he still works in to this day. The memorabilia all over this shop comes from films he worked and moviemaking equipment he collected over the years.

On any given day, you will find 2 to 3 dozen different flavors of ice cream, of which about 10 to 12 are original recipes dating back to 1919. That would include the tutti-frutti, rum-flavored ice cream with candied fruit and fresh-roasted Georgia pecans. Or the lemon custard, lemon ice cream with fresh lemon zest. They are both legendary. It all is.

When I was a kid, I used to think, man if I could ever afford all the ice cream I want to eat, that's as rich as I want to be.

—Jimmy Dean, singer

The lines move fairly quickly, and once inside there is plenty of seating for you to enjoy your scoops, but here's your insider tip on how to skip that line. If you walk inside past everyone in line, there is a cooler full of hand-packed pints right next to the cashier. If you are buying a pint, you don't have to wait in line. Grab one, pay for it, and have a seat. Or better yet, take a couple of pints to go, and walk back around the corner to Reynolds Square where you can enjoy it in true Savannah style.

6

JAVA BURRITO COMPANY

Sugar high back under control, we can make our way down to our last stop on the crawl. Continuing east on Broughton, you will pass the Trustees Theater (home of the Savannah Film Festival held every October) and a couple of other businesses. It may look like there is nothing left to see on Broughton as you stare down the street, but there is.

Crossing two tiny intersections along the way (Lincoln Street and Habersham Street), you will enter the 400 block of East Broughton. Home to the Savannah Repertory Theatre, a hair salon, and our final destination, JAVA BURRITO COMPANY, on the corner of Broughton and Price Streets.

The building dates back to the early 1900s when it served as a provisions (grocery) store in the neighborhood. Today it is home to a locally owned "build your own burrito" concept. That is in the back room. Up front is a comfortable, family-friendly front bar area where you can enjoy well-made coffees and milkshakes, plus mixed cocktails, beer, and wine.

Java Burrito is an ideal pit stop during a day of sightseeing because it offers a little bit of something for everyone.

MARTIN LUTHER KING CRAWL

1. **RANCHO ALEGRE CUBAN RESTAURANT,** 402 MLK JR. BLVD., SAVANNAH, (912) 292-1656, RANCHOALEGRECUBAN.GETBENTO.COM

2. **ORIGIN COFFEE BAR,** 356 MLK JR. BLVD., SAVANNAH, ORIGINCOFFEE.BAR, (912) 349-5122

3. **REPEAL 33,** 125 MLK JR. BLVD., SAVANNAH, (912) 200-9255, REPEAL33SAVANNAH.COM

4. **THE GREY,** 109 MLK JR. BLVD., SAVANNAH, (912) 662-5999, THEGREYRESTAURANT.COM

5. **LULU'S CHOCOLATE BAR,** 42 MLK JR. BLVD., SAVANNAH, (912) 480-4564, LULUSCHOCOLATEBAR.COM

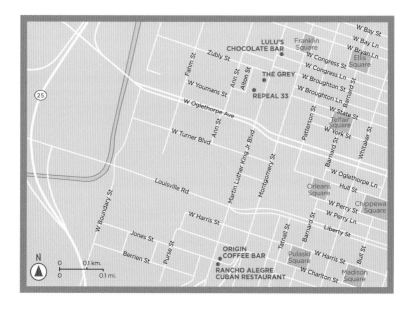

I was a drum major for peace, justice and righteousness.

—Martin Luther King Jr.

Martin Luther King

The Gateway to Savannah

For a significant portion of Savannah's history, the street formerly known as West Broad served as a cultural and business center for Savannah's African American community. Originally home to Irish Catholics and Jewish immigrants settling in Savannah, it grew in popularity immediately following the Civil War as freedmen made their way to the Georgia and South Carolina coastline and the seventh-largest city in the South at the time.

One of Savannah's railroad terminals, Union Station, once sat where the Interstate 16 overpass now enters the city. By the early 1900s, West Broad had become a hub for black-owned businesses in the region.

Today, the street is named for Dr. Martin Luther King Jr. It is the Historic District of Savannah's western border. As you look to the west from MLK Jr. Boulevard, the neighborhood becomes increasingly industrial, another reminder of Savannah's history as a port city.

Development along this corridor has grown more slowly than the rest of the Historic District, but it is coming along just the same—with several of Savannah's most popular venues choosing to call MLK Jr. Boulevard home.

1

RANCHO ALEGRE CUBAN RESTAURANT

If someone didn't tell you as much, it would be hard to imagine a Cuban restaurant stealing the hearts of the general population in Savannah, Georgia. But Rancho Alegre most certainly has. Rancho has been serving Savannah for over two decades.

It is a draw for multiple reasons. The first, of course, is the food. Cuban classics like black beans and rice, yuca frita, and lechón asado (marinated roasted pork) are staples on this menu and very popular.

RANCHO ALEGRE is possibly the first place to consider in Savannah when you want live music with your meal. Latin Jazz combos are regularly featured on the permanent stage in their dining room. If you are looking for a Friday or Saturday night party, you will find one here.

As you begin your crawl, I recommend their Cuban sandwich, served on authentic Cuban bread regularly brought in from La Segunda Bakery in Tampa. The fried green plantains (tostones) are a delightful snack paired with their house-made sangria. Personally, I am partial to their vaca frita, beef flank steak marinated in garlic, olive oil, and lime and seared with crispy edges on a flat top. A perfect cross section of my own childhood.

2 ORIGIN COFFEE BAR

Directly across Jones Street from Rancho Alegre is one of downtown Savannah's newest coffee experiences. ORIGIN COFFEE BAR was founded by Matt and Elise Higgins as a coffee catering company, specializing in private events. They soon found themselves a spot to brew regularly and eventually took the plunge to full-blown brick and mortar. Their shop is very popular serving not only well made coffees but delicious bites as well. A great way to start your day in a part of downtown that is underserved in the coffee department.

Savannah had 24 squares in its original layout. Today, there are 22.

3

REPEAL 33

Exiting Rancho Alegre and turning right (northbound) on MLK Jr. Boulevard, you will make your way 3 blocks north to Liberty Street and one of downtown Savannah's busiest intersections. Across MLK is an open green space, Battlefield Memorial Park.

Battlefield Memorial Park is the site of the Revolutionary War's Battle of Savannah in October 1779, 6 short years after settlers first arrived here. Eight hundred men died in that battle, in what became the second-deadliest fight in that war. In the distance beyond the battlefield, you will see the smokestack coming out of the Roundhouse Railroad Museum, which is open to the public.

Our tour continues on that same side of MLK Jr. Boulevard past the Savannah Visitor Center and 2 more blocks north to the address just across Oglethorpe Avenue, **REPEAL 33**.

Repeal 33 is named for the year Prohibition was repealed in America, 1933. It offers an upscale but approachable vibe and some of the best bites in Savannah. The cocktail program here also ranks near the top of the list for those in the know, featuring quite possibly the largest selection of whiskeys in Savannah. If it isn't number one, it is number two. There is no disputing that.

I've never had anything on this menu I didn't love, but it would be a failed effort if you didn't at least try their chicken wings from their starters menu. Charred wings with a Memphis dry rub, sweet vinegar, bleu cheese ranch, and a carrot-chili emulsion. There would be a protest on the streets of Savannah if they ever pulled this item off their menu. Yes, it is that good. You should try it along with maybe some oysters and a classic Old Fashioned. The 5-course chef's progressive tasting menu is also one of Savannah's most popular, offered alone, or with a wine pairing.

Savannah was the first "planned" city in the United States. Upon his arrival in 1733, General James Oglethorpe made slavery illegal. The State of Georgia reversed that decision in 1751.

4

THE GREY

There is enough to say about **THE GREY** restaurant to fill a couple of chapters in this book, but we will try to keep it brief. Headed by Beard Award–winning chef Mashama Bailey, the Grey has captured the hearts of not just Savannah but also America with their unique spin on modern Southern cuisine.

The building was once Savannah's Greyhound bus station, with a lot of original art deco details restored and preserved, giving the main dining room a near picture-perfect peek into Savannah's civil rights era and the buses that sat just outside their doors, moving passengers to and from the city.

Unless you are planning ahead, the Grey could be Savannah's toughest ticket for dinner. No fear, the front room at the Grey, entirely visible from the street, is their Diner Bar. It once served as the bus station's waiting room. Today it makes for a perfect pit stop to enjoy a tray of oysters, maybe a shrimp cocktail or a cheese plate paired with a selection from their very carefully curated wine list, or a craft cocktail. Just make sure you save room for dessert at our next stop.

5

LULU'S CHOCOLATE BAR

As you exit the Grey and continue northbound a block or so, you will reach the headwaters of Broughton Street on the right. Just ahead of you on the left is Savannah's Ships of the Sea Maritime Museum, dedicated to the ships and antiques of the Atlantic trade era of the 18th and 19th centuries.

You will cross MLK Jr. Boulevard at Broughton, but continue northbound for half a block until you reach our final destination.

LULU'S CHOCOLATE BAR is very simply Savannah's original dessert bar. Headed by two ladies who took a chance on this otherwise empty corridor over a decade ago, they combined their baking and business acumen to create a locally owned venue that remains unique on Savannah's culinary landscape: desserts and cocktails, both of which are regularly considered among the city's best.

Their flavors rotate semiregularly, so it's hard to promise you something that you may not find there, but generally it is fair to count on an appearance by their double chocolate peanut butter pie or the Lulu's Signature Strawberry Suspension cake: two layers of rum-brushed chocolate cake, mascarpone cheese, and strawberries inside.

Lulu's is also home to maybe my favorite espresso martini in Savannah, a perfect match for those treats.

WHITAKER STREET CORRIDOR CRAWL

1. **LADY AND SONS,** 102 W. CONGRESS ST., SAVANNAH, (912) 233-2600, LADYANDSONS.COM

2. **BAR BUBBLY,** 38 WHITAKER ST., SAVANNAH, (912) 224-1400

3. **FLOCK TO THE WOK,** 37 WHITAKER ST., SAVANNAH (912) 239-6697, FLOCKTOTHEWOK.COM

4. **CIRCA 1875,** 48 WHITAKER ST., SAVANNAH, (912) 433-1875, CIRCA1875.COM

5. **TEQUILA'S TOWN MEXICAN RESTAURANT,** 109 WHITAKER ST., SAVANNAH, (912) 236-2222, TEQUILASTOWN.COM

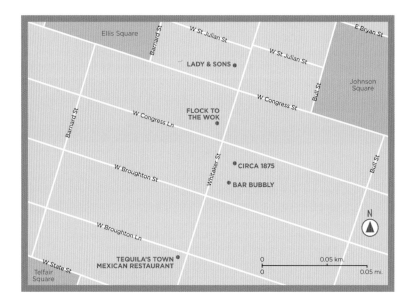

Whitaker Street Corridor

"We Really Could Fit a Lot into a Little Bit"

A few crawls ago, at Ellis Square, we explained that this section of downtown Savannah was, without question, its most active and features its highest density of restaurants and bars to enjoy along the way. Whitaker Street serves as the eastern border of that center of activity. It stretches from Bay Street for 2 miles to the Starland District, which we will discuss in a later crawl.

The downtown section of the Whitaker Street corridor, though, shouldn't be ignored. It is home to a few of Savannah's most popular eateries, jam packed together as well as dining spots for the locals who want to come downtown without getting too close to the much higher octane you will find around the corner at Ellis Square. Close, but not too close.

> Whitaker Street is one of the few streets that runs the length of the Savannah Historic District and Victorian District. It is the western border of Forsyth Park.

1 LADY AND SONS

Beginning your crawl at Bay Street, you will make your way south along Whitaker Street 2 tiny blocks past the Tiffany Taylor Art Gallery and a pizzeria to the corner of Whitaker and Congress. Once upon a time, this intersection looked like Times Square on New Year's Eve with folks standing out front waiting for their turn to dine with the Lady. Of course, we are referring to celebrity chef Paula Deen.

These days, a table is much easier to grab at **LADY AND SONS**. Their selection of Southern classic dishes like fried chicken, macaroni and cheese, and collard greens remains a draw for nostalgic types looking for a taste of Grandma's house.

The menu is served family-style (read: all you care to eat), but that doesn't preclude you from making your way up to their second-floor bar for a quick sampling of some of Paula's fried green tomatoes, served with a roasted red pepper sauce and sweet onion relish and a Honey and Pear Margarita. Me? I'd ask if I could purchase an individual dessert. All these years later, I'd put Paula's Ooey Gooey Butter Cake or her banana pudding up against anything you will find in this city.

Paula Deen's Lady and Sons existed in two other Savannah locations before moving to their current spot on Whitaker at Congress Street. Paula got her start delivering bag lunches to the business crowd around Savannah, billing herself as "the Bag Lady."

2 BAR BUBBLY

Stepping back out onto Whitaker Street, you will see maybe Savannah's busiest single-lane intersection, Whitaker and Congress. Proceed with caution as you make your way across Congress and Whitaker to the opposite corner, home to a real estate office. Once you've taken a peek at how valuable property is around here, step one building over to our next stop, Bar Bubbly.

BAR BUBBLY gets a stop on this crawl, frankly, because it is Savannah's only champagne bar. Of course you can find bubbles practically anywhere, but you won't find a greater selection of reasonably priced sparkling wines anywhere downtown. Yes, there are a couple of selections for the connoisseurs, but Bar Bubbly is more geared toward a younger demographic looking to down their body weight in bottomless mimosas. Not that there is anything wrong with that.

There is no food to speak of, but they will allow you to bring in food from outside so you can enjoy a nice cava or sparkling rosé. Not hungry? No problem, you will want to be at our next stop across the street.

When I read about the evils of drinking, I gave up reading.
—Henny Youngman, American comedian

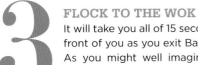

3 FLOCK TO THE WOK

It will take you all of 15 seconds to find our next stop: directly in front of you as you exit Bar Bubbly back onto Whitaker Street. As you might well imagine, the dinner rush can get pretty crowded on this block with several excellent options within feet of each other. But our next stop is right across the street.

FLOCK TO THE WOK offers modern Asian cuisine, but from our seat, it's our version of "American-style" Chinese food. Favorites like General Tso chicken, Mongolian beef, and kung pao chicken dot the menu, along with noodles and fried rice options.

Not to be missed are the dumplings. Pan seared or steamed. If you catch them at the right time of day, you will see them being made by hand in the window along Whitaker Street. The soup dumplings some Savannahians will swear by. Particularly the pork and crab dumplings. If you can grab a seat, you can eat a little or a lot. All of it good.

Not be ignored is Flock's speakeasy "Peacock Lounge" located in their basement. The entryway is off the lane behind where the restaurant is located. Peacock is one of Savannah's most "Instagrammable" bars. The décor is impeccable, trendy, and dark, featuring neon accents and a faux fireplace. The clientele is usually an interesting mix of ages featuring both tourists and locals. Everyone loves Peacock and for very good reason. It's a perfect spot for a nightcap.

4

CIRCA 1875

Leaving Flock to the Wok and/or Peacock Lounge, you are now back out on Whitaker Street at Congress Lane. Our next stop takes you from Asian to French: directly ahead and to your right, at **CIRCA 1875**.

Circa 1875, very simply, is one of Savannah's favorite local gathering spots. We phrase it that way deliberately because there is a lot going on here. On one side, you have their dimly lit gastropub featuring dark wood accents and tiny nooks for privacy (if you are looking for some).

Next door—but also connected at the back of the room—is their full-service brasserie, and one of Savannah's toughest seats to grab if you don't have a reservation.

The good news is the full menu is available on either side of the restaurant or gastropub. So you can pick a side, depending on how much time you have or want to invest. The list of wines by the glass was named Savannah's best several times featuring predominantly European options. So there is definitely something great waiting for you to pair with their already famous cheeseboard or a serving of escargot, served piping hot, and just dripping with garlic and butter.

5

TEQUILA'S TOWN MEXICAN RESTAURANT

Back out onto Whitaker Street, the restaurant you see directly in front of you is worth a mention: Persepolis offers Mediterranean cuisine and is one of Savannah's under-the-radar eating establishments. Save that one for another day.

Instead, our crawl will continue south to the corner of Whitaker and Broughton Streets, home to the Paris Market, one of Savannah's most beautiful shopping venues.

Crossing over Broughton Street and continuing down Whitaker directly ahead, you will see New Realm Brewing Company's Savannah location. New Realm is based in Atlanta, and features a variety of craft beers and house-made spirits. Our last stop, though, is a visit with a properly made margarita, along with a healthy bowl of chips and salsa directly across the street at **TEQUILA'S TOWN**.

There are several options for Mexican food in Savannah, with Tequila's Town offering three locations across the city. This one on Whitaker is their only space in the heart of downtown.

Featuring an extended list of over 100 agave spirits, including their own private label, Tequila's Town is regularly named a Savannah favorite. The gua-

camole here is freshly prepared tableside, yes, every single time. That ensures its freshness and yes, it is delicious. As is most everything on the menu here.

BULL STREET NORTH CRAWL

1. **WRIGHT SQUARE BISTRO,** 21 W. YORK ST., SAVANNAH, (912) 238-1150, WRIGHTSQUARECAFE.COM

2. **THE COLLINS QUARTER,** 151 BULL ST., SAVANNAH, (912) 777-4147, THECOLLINSQUARTER.COM

3. **THE GALLERY ESPRESSO,** 234 BULL ST., SAVANNAH, (912) 233-5348, GALLERYESPRESSO.COM

4. **SIX PENCE PUB,** 245 BULL ST., SAVANNAH, (912) 233-3156, SIXPENCEPUB.COM

5. **ARTILLERY BAR,** 307 BULL ST., SAVANNAH, (912) 335-5200, ARTILLERYBAR.COM

6. **GRYPHON,** 337 BULL ST., SAVANNAH, (912) 525-5880, SCADGRYPHON.COM

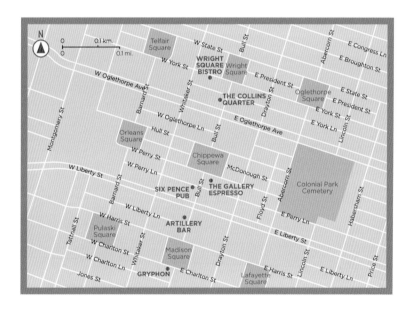

Bull Street North

Straight through the Heart of Town

While New York has its Broadway and Chicago flexes its Michigan Avenue, here in tiny downtown Savannah, Georgia, we boast . . . Bull Street. Future governor of South Carolina William Bull assisted General James Oglethorpe in laying out the now famous city grid that would later become Savannah. Bull Street runs directly through the center of our National Historic Landmark District.

Beginning at Bay Street at the foot of Savannah City Hall, Bull Street runs through 5 city squares all the way to Forsyth Park. It then continues on the other side of the park for a few more miles through the heart of Savannah's very much up-and-coming Starland District, which we will visit in a later crawl.

Along this northern stretch of Bull Street between city hall and the park, you will find a wonderful mix of history, architecture, charm, and of course food and drink. Most of it is tree covered, making it one of Savannah's most popular strolls.

1

WRIGHT SQUARE BISTRO

Beginning at the intersection of Bay and Congress Streets you may notice you are surrounded by banks. Johnson Square is nicknamed "Bankers Square" because of that, but that is hardly the most interesting thing about this particular square.

If you look up at the live oak trees that envelop the square, what you won't see is one of the things that this square has become known for: the lack of Spanish moss hanging from any branch in the square. Some would like you to believe public lynchings were held in this square.

Many others refer to any series of paranormal events connected in some way to the square. Every other tree-covered square in Savannah has moss hanging from those trees. Johnson Square does not. The truth? We haven't found it yet. So let's grab a bite to eat.

Make your way away from the square southbound on Bull to Wright Square just about 150 feet ahead. As you enter the square and look down State Street to the left, you see one of downtown Savannah's neighborhood Italian restaurants, Bella Napoli.

As you continue to make your way across Wright Square (named for James Wright, third and final royal governor of Georgia), you reach York Street and the bank on the corner. Crossing over Bull Street, continue west on York past several shops until you reach our next stop, **WRIGHT**

SQUARE BISTRO. Wright Square Bistro is a "catchall" type of spot—meaning there is something here for everyone.

Originally created as a tiny cafe to satisfy your sweet tooth, Wright Square has expanded over the years into a two-sided eatery. One side still focuses on your grab-and-go-type bites, sweet and savory. But the other side has evolved as a seating area to enjoy a full lunch or an early dinner.

The menu changes somewhat regularly, but there are items they cannot pull without repercussions from their regulars. One of them is their meatloaf, a wonderful mixture of beef, pork, spices, and bacon topped with a special house glaze. The sweets are almost entirely made by a local wholesale bakery down the street—Wicked Cakes. Because they are. Flavors change regularly. Just go with it and grab one.

TIP

If you can catch him there, the hot dog cart at Johnson Square (at the beginning of the Bull Street North crawl) is one of downtown Savannah's best-kept secrets.

2 THE COLLINS QUARTER

Back out onto York Street, we will turn right and continue down to Bull Street and turn right again. We are now making our way southbound on Bull. At the other end of the block, literally around the corner from where we started, we arrive at Savannah's crown jewel of brunch: the Collins Quarter.

THE COLLINS QUARTER opened in the summer of 2014, at a time when there just weren't that many options for brunch in Savannah, much less outside of a Sunday morning. Named for a gathering place between office buildings in Melbourne, Australia, the Collins Quarter has established itself as one of the Savannah brunch scene's most appealing locales. The 60-to-90-minute wait you will likely encounter on the weekends will tell you all you need to know about that.

The food is fabulous and consistent. The coffee program could be Savannah's richest for a sit-down restaurant. Similarly, the champagne list at the Collins Quarter is the largest in the city. And yes, we said champagne. Not sparkling wine. Sometimes that matters.

Oh, but what to eat? The Moroccan Scramble featuring merguez lamb sausage, chickpeas, scrambled eggs, Fresno chiles, and avocado is one of my personal go-tos here. Not that hungry? Sit at the counter and enjoy a spiced lavender mocha. The Collins Quarter put lavender mochas on the map here, and it is now one of their most popular. If you are looking for something stronger, I might consider the Gin and Roses. Basil-infused gin, lemon, secret sweetness, and sparkling rosé.

We should mention that the Collins Quarter is the flagship location for a series of restaurants across town. Including a second Collins Quarter in the middle of Forsyth Park; plus the Fitzroy, a popular gastropub on Drayton Street; and Ukiyo, a Japanese street food restaurant that we will visit on a later crawl.

We should also mention that because brunch is so popular here at the Collins Quarter, their dinner service doesn't get nearly the play that it should. It is very good, featuring a glowing candle-lit dining room once the sun goes down. Add it to your short list.

3

THE GALLERY ESPRESSO

Once again on Bull Street, at the corner of Bull and Oglethorpe Avenue, we begin to make our way across the street to the median. Once there, you can look back across Bull from the Collins Quarter at the Juliette Gordon Low House, birthplace of the young lady who founded the Girl Scouts of America. Also up Oglethorpe Avenue, a quarter block behind the Collins Quarter, is Husk Savannah—one of Savannah's better restaurants, and home to perhaps the prettiest restaurant bar space in town.

Continuing across Bull, we make our way 1 block up to Chippewa Square. Home to the Forrest Gump bench in the movie. The bench was placed in front of you where Bull forms a T with the square on this side for the making of the movie. That bench is now in a museum down the street.

Through Chippewa Square and out the other end on the left, you find a corner coffee shop. **THE GALLERY ESPRESSO.**

The Gallery Espresso has been in Savannah since long before coffee was cool. The chairs are comfy, the coffee is strong, and the chocolate cake is divine. What's not to love? It's a perfect stop for one or both, with windows looking back out onto Bull and one of downtown Savannah's most picturesque intersections in a city full of them.

4
SIX PENCE PUB

Continuing up Bull Street, we pass Chocolat by Adam Turoni. We discussed Adam's amazing truffles in detail on our Broughton Street West crawl, his other location. Looking across Bull is the impossible-to-miss red phone booth and one of downtown Savannah's most charming Instagram moments. It just so happens to be parked outside of our next stop, SIX PENCE PUB.

Six Pence Pub is the closest thing downtown Savannah has to Cheers. You know that place where everyone knows your name and they are glad you came? Considering the fact that it is located in almost the exact center of Savannah's Historic District, it is heavily trafficked by locals. It could be the fact that it is maybe the only spot in this part of town where one can grab a proper pint.

The space is charming; the service is always good. The selection of beers on tap is impressive, and then there is the conversation. You are just as likely to be sitting next to someone who came in from Maryland specifically for their roast beef platter as you are an employee from the hotel across the street who just left work. All of that and everything in between. That's Six Pence. Enjoy a cold one, tell Sandra we said hello, and make your way back out to Bull Street.

Bull Street from city hall to Liberty Street represents the final home stretch for Savannah's St. Patrick's Day parade. The parade route ends at Madison Square, just beyond Liberty Street.

5

ARTILLERY BAR

Continuing up Bull half a block, you reach Liberty Street and the heart of Savannah's Historic District. To your left, towering above the intersection, is the historic DeSoto Hotel. Immediately ahead on the right is Public Kitchen and Bar. We will visit both locations and many more along Liberty Street during our Liberty Street crawl.

Just beyond Liberty and Public Kitchen, one of Public's sister properties is a spot for something stronger than beer if you are up for it. **ARTILLERY BAR,** Savannah's most beautiful pure cocktail bar.

Artillery is a nod to the Georgia Hussars, a historical cavalry unit founded before the Revolutionary War. A purely volunteer militia, they kept their artillery in a building where this cocktail bar currently sits.

There's no sugarcoating Artillery. It is warm and inviting, because this is Savannah after all, but it isn't the kind of place you walk in looking for a pitcher of beer or a few chicken wings. Artillery serves a niche in Savannah and serves it well.

Classic cocktails, wine, bubbles, and some beers are what you will find in a setting that rivals any in the big city.

Incidentally, the Georgia Hussars unit continues to this day as a part of the Georgia National Guard.

6

GRYPHON

As you continue along Bull Street, you will make your way through Madison Square, named for James Madison, the fourth president of the United States. We reach a point along the northern stretch of Bull Street where the number of commercial establishments drops dramatically. In fact, there is only one eatery between Madison Square and Forsyth Park 8 blocks to the south. It's just on the other side of the square on your right headed south: **THE GRYPHON TEA ROOM.**

TIP

Savannah is incredibly dog friendly. Practically any restaurant with outdoor seating would be more than willing to bring you a bowl of cold water for your pup.

The Gryphon Tea Room is owned and operated by the Savannah College of Art and Design. The building opened in 1923. This corner space served as an apothecary for much of its existence until 1998, when it was converted into this tea room.

Inside you find stained-glass light fixtures and mahogany bookcases, making for a perfect setting for an afternoon tea.

Beyond their selection of teas, you can find a selection of nonalcoholic specialty drinks, plus coffees. There is a food menu featuring sandwiches and salads. If you are looking for an afternoon tea, they offer a selection of tea sandwiches, scones, pastries, and petit fours for roughly $20 per person. A beautiful way to spend an afternoon.

JONES STREET CRAWL

1. **CLARY'S CAFE,** 404 ABERCORN ST. (AT JONES), SAVANNAH, (912) 233-0402, CLARYSCAFE.COM

2. **MRS. WILKES DINING ROOM,** 107 W. JONES ST., SAVANNAH, (912) 232-5997, MRSWILKES.COM

3. **CRYSTAL BEER PARLOR,** 301 W. JONES ST., SAVANNAH, (912) 349-1000, CRYSTALBEERPARLOR.COM

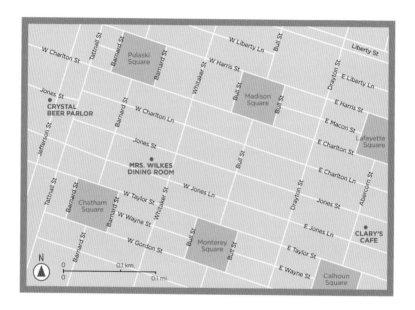

JONES STREET is one of Savannah's prettiest and most visited streets, but—considering the amount of traffic it sees—it is also among its most quiet.

Jones Street

Savannah's Residential Street

Jones Street, named for Major John Jones, an officer in the Revolutionary War, remains downtown Savannah's most prestigious address. It is also Savannah's widest downtown street and its most picturesque downtown street. I'm obviously not at liberty to divulge any names, but I will say if a celebrity decided to call downtown Savannah home, then there is a good chance they are setting up shop on Jones Street. I don't know if any remain today, but I can say that a few have lived along Jones in the past.

Most of the homes here were built in the 1850s and 1860s.

Spanning roughly 9 tree-covered blocks in length, Jones Street has something new to share on every visit. It says a lot about a street and the restaurants on it when you dedicate an entire crawl to only three stops. But if you know Savannah, then you know. The three we are going to share are locked in as Savannah classic must-visits. You are about to see why.

> Several bed-and-breakfast inns dot Savannah's prettiest residential street, making it one of the most desirable areas for visitors to stay while in Savannah.

1

CLARY'S CAFE

If you choose to start your crawl at the eastern end of Jones at Broad Street, you will enjoy a few blocks of beautiful homes before you reach our first stop. There are no turns; there are no hidden entrances. Just make your way westbound on Jones until you reach Abercorn Street. Sitting right there on the corner is your mid-Jones oasis: Savannah's most popular diner, CLARY'S CAFE.

Clary's began as a drugstore in the 1930s. Later it was a soda shop and a diner. Its star shot over the moon once it was featured prominently in the 1997 film *Midnight in the Garden of Good and Evil*.

During peak times of the year, it is not uncommon to see a crowd gathered outside of Clary's Cafe waiting on a table. It's a straightforward approach here: breakfast and lunch featuring pancakes, eggs, omelets, and toast early, sandwiches, salads, burgers, and ice cream sundaes midday. It is your classic greasy spoon and there's not a person out there who doesn't love it.

If you are there early, try the Elvis: thick-sliced french toast stuffed with peanut butter and bananas. Passing through midday, you might enjoy the Philly cheesesteak, served—like all sandwiches—with french fries.

Of course, if you overdo it at Clary's, there's a more than good chance you will regret that decision once you reach the next spot.

MRS. WILKES DINING ROOM

One good thing about a crawl dedicated to a single street is, the directions are easy. Leaving Clary's Cafe, cross over Abercorn Street and continue westbound on Jones. Once you travel 3 blocks, you will arrive at the intersection of Jones and Whitaker Streets, home to the Whitaker Street Design District, some of Savannah's most exclusive boutique shopping. Cross over Whitaker and make your way about half a block and you reach **MRS. WILKES DINING ROOM**. Though you are very likely to see a gaggle of hungry visitors long before you hit the front door.

On another crawl, I refer to Savannah's Olde Pink House as the most popular culinary destination in the city. If that one isn't, then this one is.

Mrs. Wilkes Dining Room got its start way back in 1943 when a young lady named Sema Wilkes took over an already established boardinghouse. Her plan was to offer a place to stay upstairs and good comfort food downstairs. That was the formula then and it is largely the formula today.

Visitors regularly line up along Jones Street before the doors open just to make efficient use of their time. It is fair to say 90 percent of the year there is a line to dine at Mrs. Wilkes. The good news is, Jones Street is protected by trees and, as we mentioned, one of Savannah's most beautiful destinations. The menu for the day is posted at the front door on a chalkboard. Choices always include their classic fried chicken and one other protein, maybe meatloaf or beef stew. Beyond that there are several vegetable sides, including butter beans and creamed corn and a couple of desserts.

Once inside, groups are seated family-style at rounds of 10. Yes, right alongside people you may not have known before, but become friendly with while you were all in line together.

As soon as you are seated, there is no ordering or choosing. Everything you saw on that menu at the door comes flying out of the kitchen and is dropped onto your table.

This is the epitome of family-style eating. Passing plates while engaging in conversation. Serving bowls empty? Let one of the servers know and they'll bring you another. It's that simple. I can't recommend anything, really, because it is all mouthwatering delicious.

In between dining rooms is a wall full of photographs with celebrities who have shared a meal at Mrs. Wilkes. Names like Charlize Theron, Kevin Spacey, Walter Cronkite, Liam Neeson, and Barack Obama. Those are just a few.

Once you are done with your meal, you pay at the door. Mrs. Wilkes has always been cash only, no cards at all. They do have an ATM on-site, or will gladly accept a payment via Venmo. They are only open Monday through Friday 11 a.m. to 2 p.m. Yes, lunch only.

3 CRYSTAL BEER PARLOR

If you continue to the end of the block on Jones Street, you reach Barnard Street, cross over, and reach what seems like a Jones Street dead end at Tattnall Street. Have no fear, just make a right and then your first left and you are still on Jones, where you will continue 1 very short block to 301 Jones Street and the **CRYSTAL BEER PARLOR**.

The building now home to Crystal Beer Parlor dates back to the early 1900s when it was a grocery store. In the 1930s it became an eatery and, according to some, was one of the first places in America to serve alcohol after Prohibition was repealed in 1933.

Nearly 90 years later, and several incarnations of the Savannah classic along the way, it's now owned by a Savannah native, John Nichols. He is deserving of a mention on this crawl because of the way he came about ownership of this institution.

He grew up coming here. He remembers waiting for his dad out in the car while Dad "waited on a sack of burgers to take home." Years later, he grew up to become a chef and had the opportunity to buy the Crystal Beer Parlor. He threw the letter in the trash. Then thought better of it. He decided that if he was going to do it, he was going to do it right. As a tribute to Savannah, and everything the restaurant has meant to this city.

The space is a living museum with memorabilia on display everywhere. Some of it was donated by patrons, A lot of it was his own. Some of it he tracked down on the internet and purchased, just to make sure it had a proper home on display in Savannah.

Two of the rooms in the restaurant—the Whitlock Room and the Smitty Room—are named for servers who worked at CBP for nearly 45 years. The

sign on the back wall of the main dining room is original. Burgers for 5 cents? Once upon a time, yes. The tradition is rich here.

Once you navigate all of that, there is the food. All of it good. All of it popular. My go-to is their double-decker turkey club sandwich. My favorite in Savannah. The Georgia BBQ nachos are unique in that they are a pile of tortilla chips topped with pulled BBQ pork, cheddar, diced onion, jalapeno, and chopped dill pickles. The Classic Crystal Burger is a regular mention around town as being a staple as well. But really, it is all good. I have yet to have a bad meal at the Crystal Beer Parlor.

The bar lining the main dining room is original and features a very healthy selection of craft brews. Reservations are not accepted, and at peak times on the weekend you are going to wait a bit for a sit. One look inside and you will see that it is absolutely time well spent. A Savannah treasure for sure.

LIBERTY STREET CRAWL

1. **SAVANNAH COFFEE ROASTERS,** 215 W. LIBERTY ST., SAVANNAH,
   (912) 352-2994, SAVANNAHCOFFEE.COM

2. **FRANKLIN'S / PUBLIC KITCHEN AND BAR,** 5 W. LIBERTY ST., SAVANNAH,
   (912) 200-4045, ILOVEFRANKLINS.COM

3. **THE DESOTO SAVANNAH HOTEL,** 15 E. LIBERTY ST., SAVANNAH,
   (912) 232-9000, THEDESOTOSAVANAH.COM

4. **SAVOY SOCIETY,** 102 E. LIBERTY ST., SUITE #109, SAVANNAH,
   (912) 662-6665, SAVOYSOCIETY.COM

5. **MIRABELLE,** 343 ABERCORN ST., SAVANNAH, (912) 231-3936,
   MIRABELLESAVANNAH.COM

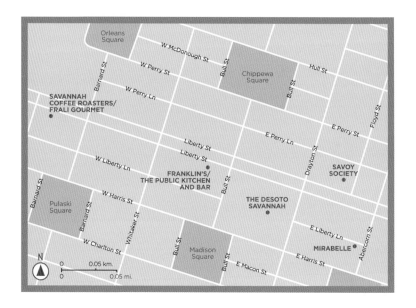

Liberty Street

"Most Likely to Find a Local"

Liberty Street is one of downtown Savannah's primary east–west corridors. It features a solid selection of not only restaurants and bars but also hotels, bed-and-breakfasts, and shopping. It is also—unofficially—considered by locals to be something of a southern border to the far more active downtown district to the north.

The area to the south of Liberty Street becomes primarily, though not exclusively, residential. That is why when local residents come out to play, you are more likely to find them somewhere along Liberty Street. It also runs along the side of the Savannah Civic Center and the Johnny Mercer Theatre, which makes Liberty Street one of downtown Savannah's most popular destinations for a preshow meal or a postshow beverage.

1

SAVANNAH COFFEE ROASTERS

Beginning our crawl toward the western end of Liberty Street at Tattnall, you see the civic center and its parking lot across the street. Considering the history around here, that venue is fairly new. It was built in 1974 and up until early 2022 was Savannah's primary venue for concerts. In February 2022, the brand-new Enmarket Arena opened its doors a mile or so away. Back on this side of Liberty you will find Savannah's largest coffee shop, **SAVANNAH COFFEE ROASTERS**.

Savannah Coffee Roasters was first established in 1909 on Bay Street here in downtown Savannah. In those 100-plus years it has grown and expanded, moved, and then moved again before settling in this spot on Liberty Street close to a decade ago.

Inside you will find a comfortable seating area before arriving at a true "working" cafe. You see, the beans are roasted in a couple of rooms in the back. Those rooms surround the kitchen, which is generally a beehive of activity preparing fresh snacks and sandwiches for their customers. Along the walls are any number of varietals of coffee beans for sale and other retail items.

TIP

Right next door to the beginning of our crawl at Savannah Coffee Roasters is **FraLi Gourmet** (217 W. Liberty St., Savannah, 912-234-4644, fraligourmet.com), an Italian pasta maker and eatery. One of Savannah's better values for a freshly made inexpensive lunch.

The baked goods here are always wonderful. The chocolate chip cookies make a strong case for my favorites in the city. Sandwiches are prepared on freshly baked breads as well, offering you a perfect first stop on your crawl.

2 FRANKLIN'S / PUBLIC KITCHEN AND BAR

Stepping out from Savannah Coffee and to the right, you continue eastbound on Liberty Street into a largely residential section of the corridor. Crossing Barnard Street, you see the Stephen Williams House to the left across the street. Just ahead on the right is the Inn at West Liberty, both of which are charming places to stay in Savannah.

Crossing Whitaker Street and beyond Mellow Mushroom Pizza, you find our next stop, another ideal location for a morning latte and pastry: FRANKLIN'S.

Franklin's is relatively new to Savannah but very quickly has become one of Savannah's most delicious hideaways, offering coffees and pastries, as well as several items for brunch. Franklin's outdoor cafe seating makes it the ideal spot for your historic Savannah Instagram breakfast and coffee.

The croque monsieur is what I usually get when I walk in here. Their creole mustard béchamel makes for an unforgettable experience. But don't pass on a cup of their tomato basil bisque. It is Savannah's most famous soup. How good is it? When the restaurant across the street was sold to the current owners, the recipe for the bisque was part of the deal. Savannahians crave it in the winter. It is that good.

On the coffee side come some of the Savannah's most talked about creations. The Spicy Mocha with cayenne, chili powder, cinnamon, cocoa powder, and milk is excellent. As is their horchata latte with honey, vanilla, nutmeg, cinnamon, and coconut milk. There is also a selection of coffee-based cocktails if—of course—you are ready to turn your late-morning dial to medium high.

While most of the charm is out on the sidewalk, there is also indoor seating at Franklin's. It connects inside with their sister restaurant, **PUBLIC KITCHEN AND BAR**. Franklin's handles the morning and early afternoon; Public opens for lunch, dinner, and later. Depending on what time of day you are making your way through, either is a worthy stop on your crawl.

3 THE DESOTO SAVANNAH HOTEL

On a previous crawl, we took you through the Marshall House, one of Savannah's oldest hotels. That said, it would be impossible not to do the same with our next stop, directly across Bull Street from our previous. The **DESOTO SAVANNAH HOTEL** takes up the entire next block.

Built in 1890, the DeSoto was once "the center of all social life" in Savannah. It has hosted several presidents as well as celebrities from Hollywood's golden age, such as Katharine Hepburn and Gregory Peck. Elvis Presley and Michael Jackson also stayed at the DeSoto at one point.

A stroll through the lobby gives you a peek at some of that history. The chandeliers above your head all date to 1890. The historical details are everywhere, with a corner of the lobby dedicated to the DeSoto's place in Savannah's journey.

At the back of the room you find the 1540 Room, which was for decades a central gathering spot for locals to enjoy a proper Sunday brunch. Today it is a fine dining venue, inspired by the flavors of North Africa and the Mediterranean. Our stop today, though, takes us to the left toward Proof and Provisions and their covered veranda just outside.

The elevated outdoor seating area along Liberty Street at P&P offers a perfect respite from the elements. It offers a full liquor bar, wines by the glass, and local beers, any of which will fit this scene perfectly as you look out onto Liberty Street and get a solid peek at daily life in Savannah.

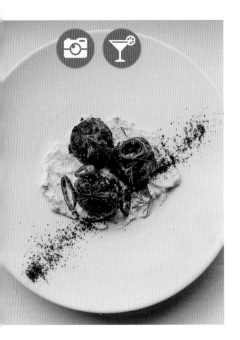

When the DeSoto Savannah Hotel opened on New Year's Day in 1890, it featured a swimming pool, a solarium, a soda shop, a barber shop, and a lighted miniature golf course.

4

SAVOY SOCIETY

Once again out on Liberty in front of the DeSoto, we turn right and continue across Drayton Street. At the corner of Drayton and Liberty we find Treylor Park–Hitch, which we discussed in detail during our Bay Street crawl.

Once again crossing Liberty Street to the north, we arrive at the opposite corner and the foot of Drayton Tower, a residential building. Our crawl takes us east up Liberty Street to the other end of this building and the glass box that is Savoy Society.

SAVOY SOCIETY is one of downtown Savannah's most popular destinations for locals. It's top three easily, but there are more than three reasons why.

For starters, it's a proper cocktail bar. Some of Savannah's best bar talent calls Savoy home. Beyond that, there is the food. That includes the shareables like the charcuterie board or spicy pimento cheese plate (you are in the South, y'all). Or quick snacks like the very popular Crispy Spam Slider. That guy comes in at under 3 bucks. Keeping Savannah's vegetarian population in mind, there are several options across the board, which could be enticing to a particular diet.

Flatbreads and other sandwiches fill in the menu and are a great accompaniment to the scene. During the day, the soundtrack is vinyl spinning in the corner; if you behave, the bartender may let you pick the next selection from their wall of choices. Deeper into the night, particularly on the weekends, you may find a DJ spinning in the corner.

5

MIRABELLE

Returning to Liberty Street and turning to the left, we reach the corner of Liberty and Abercorn Streets. If you look to the left about half a block ahead, you can see the wrought iron railing that borders Savannah's Colonial Park Historic Cemetery. How much history will you find over there? It became a park in 1896, a full 43 years *after* they stopped burying people there. Look it up; it's a fascinating visit.

The Cathedral Basilica of St. John the Baptist in Savannah was dedicated in 1876. The actual parish was first created by immigrants fleeing Haiti and France in the late 1700s.

Our crawl, however, takes us to the right, once again crossing Liberty Street headed south. On the diagonal corner you will see St. Vincent's Academy, Savannah's all-female Catholic school. Beyond that and impossible to miss are the twin spires of the Cathedral Basilica of St. John the Baptist. Continue for half a block and on the right you will find our next stop: **MIRABELLE**.

Mirabelle is aptly named for views of the bells across the street at the cathedral. Mirabelle is tiny. Make that very tiny, with a few seats inside and a few more outside. The menu features a few different freshly made waffles topped with maybe something sweet like peach cobbler or a lemon lavender curd cream or something savory like ham, melted swiss, and a black pepper béchamel. Either way, you will enjoy.

Grab a coffee, maybe split a snack, and enjoy the view. That is why you are here. It is spectacular. Afterward, cross the street and make your way through the cathedral. It is usually open to the public and one of Savannah's most popular places to visit.

TIP

Randy's BBQ sits on Liberty Street about halfway beyond the Historic District's eastern border— Broad Street. At Broad, Liberty becomes Wheaton Street. Randy's is a "roadside stand" that opens only for lunch and is cash only. They don't have a phone or website, but you can find them easily with an internet search.

DRAYTON STREET CORRIDOR CRAWL

1. **THE ORIGINAL PINKIE MASTERS BAR,** 318 DRAYTON ST., SAVANNAH, (912) 999-7106, THEORIGINALPINKIES.COM

2. **BURRITOS PANTANO,** 14 DRAYTON ST., SAVANNAH, (912) 695-0836, BURRITOSPANTANOSAV.COM

3. **ZUNZIBAR,** 236 DRAYTON ST., SAVANNAH, (912) 298-0761, ZUNZIBAR.COM

4. **EMPORIUM KITCHEN AND WINE MARKET / PERRY LANE HOTEL,** 256 E. PERRY LN., SAVANNAH, (912) 415-9000, EMPORIUMSAVANNAH.COM

5. **MCDONOUGH'S RESTAURANT & LOUNGE,** 21 E. MCDONOUGH ST., SAVANNAH, (912) 233-6136, MCDONOUGHSLOUNGE.COM

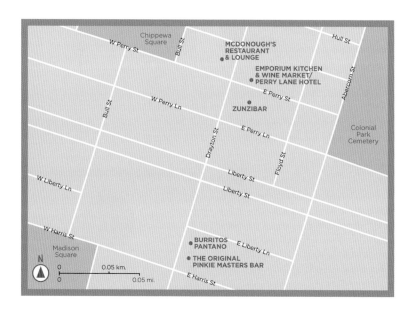

Drayton Street Corridor

The Kinda/Sorta Bar Crawl

Drayton Street, and Whitaker Street a couple of blocks up, are two of downtown Savannah's primary streets for going the longest distance without the burden of navigating one of our squares. For that reason, they are both very popular. They each run one way. Whitaker runs southbound from Bay Street. Drayton Street runs one way northbound to Bay.

This crawl is small, 3 blocks long, but most of the places we will take you to are landmarks in Savannah, so they should not be ignored. The crawl starts with Savannah's most famous dive bar and ends at our most famous karaoke bar. There is food worthy of a stop along the way, but this crawl is a little higher octane than the others. User discretion is advised.

1 THE ORIGINAL PINKIE MASTERS BAR

Our crawl begins at Drayton and Harris Streets, 1 block south of Liberty Street and in the shadow of the DeSoto Savannah Hotel.

When I travel, I love to play a game where I ask everyday folks I meet where I should go while I am in their city. The question is generally phrased "You haven't been to [insert name of city] until you've been to . . ." As soon as I get three or four of the same answer, then I know where to go.

In Savannah, Mrs. Wilkes Dining Room probably fills in that blank for food. For drinks? I think there is only one answer: **PINKIE MASTERS**.

"Pinkies," as we call it, is a legendary dive bar. Dating back to 1953, it took on the nickname of its original owner, Luis Chris Masterpolis—"Pinkie." He was big into the political scene. His bar became a haven for cold beer and quality conversation.

Pinkies is probably most known for the urban tale that then governor of Georgia Jimmy Carter announced his candidacy for president while standing on the bar. That version of the story is close, but not entirely accurate.

As we mentioned, Pinkie was big into politics and was an early supporter of President Carter's political career. During a visit to Savannah for a function in the DeSoto Hotel across the street, President Carter decided he wanted to stop in to say hi to an old friend and supporter. The Secret Service was then tasked with getting President Carter out through the kitchen and loading docks you still see across the street and into Pinkie Masters.

Once he made it inside safely, President Carter stood up on the bar and addressed the full house, thanking Pinkie and everyone for their continued support. There is a star embedded in the bar to mark the spot where President Carter stood.

On any given night at Pinkies you'll find perhaps Savannah's best cross section of locals. Shorts and flip-flops or evening gowns and tuxedos after a night at the ballet. They all know where to gather. Pinkie Masters is cash only. There is an ATM inside.

2

BURRITOS PANTANO

Unfortunately, Pinkies doesn't offer any food, but thankfully you are welcome to bring some in if you like and there's a burrito shop right next door.

BURRITOS PANTANO is not one of your run-of-the-mill "build your own" burrito joints. Not at all. Owner Patrick Zimmerman is a former fine dining chef who decided long ago to drop the pretense and just make solid, everyday food. Burritos Pantano is his spin on the authentic-type Mexican eats you are less likely to find in a tourist-centric area.

They offer baskets of chips and salsa, all of which are made in-house. The red salsa packs a spicy punch, but the avocado is maybe my favorite. There are nachos, salads, and, of course, burritos. Beginning with something simple like house-made refried beans and cheese, all the way up to Burrito #7, which includes beans, roasted chili relish, queso, potato sticks, chicharrones (pork rinds), carnitas (slow-roasted pork), and avocado salsa.

The large is generally big enough to share. Especially if you are going with chips and salsa as well. You can have a seat inside or take it all back to Pinkies and wash it down with a margarita. The choices are yours.

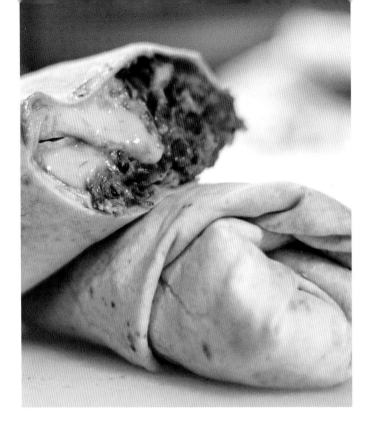

3

ZUNZIBAR

Once you've wrapped up your Pinkies-Burrito fun, you can make your way back toward Liberty Street. At the corner you will see Treylor Park-Hitch, which we discussed in detail on our Bay Street crawl.

Crossing over Liberty Street and continuing for 1 very short block, you will come upon a white oasis accented in the colors of a beach ball. It's impossible to miss. It is called ZUNZIBAR.

Zunzibar is the franken-morphed creation that once upon a time was Zunzi's, Savannah's legendary South African–inspired sandwich shop. Zunzi's made headlines for years serving out of almost literally a hole in the wall down the road on York Street.

Their Conquistador sandwich—chicken, romaine, tomato, and provolone on French bread and topped with Zunzi's special sauce—made them famous. At one time it was named the best sandwich in the state of Georgia by a national magazine.

That sandwich remains the go-to here and is worth a try if you've never had one before. The Godfather is also a descendant of that original menu and very popular. Mix in a cocktail from their full liquor bar and enjoy the scene, at whatever speed you choose.

If the green-windowed building in front of you catches your attention as not fitting in with the rest of historic Savannah, it should. Drayton Tower was built around 1950. In 2005 it was purchased and renovated into luxury condominiums.

4 EMPORIUM KITCHEN AND WINE MARKET / PERRY LANE HOTEL

From your seat at Zunzibar it will be very easy to see our last two stops. They make up two of the four corners at the intersection you are seated at. Beginning across Perry Lane on your same side of the street, you will find **EMPORIUM KITCHEN AND WINE MARKET**.

Emporium is inside the très chic **PERRY LANE HOTEL** and serves as their restaurant. There is a separate entrance into the restaurant, at which point you will immediately see their coffee counter and ice cream coolers on the right. To the left you will find their U-shaped bar with plenty of seating for either in between.

The glass that surrounds the bar makes for a fishbowl effect when people watching outside on very busy Drayton Street. During a hot Savannah summer, I'd much rather be in here nursing some rosé than out there.

The ice cream? Leopold's finest—without the long line. How about that?

Two other stops in this building to consider: the rooftop here is called Peregrin, one of Savannah's most scenic rooftop venues. We discuss it more in our Savannah Rooftop section. Also, the Wayward Lounge in the back of the building. Home of Savannah's best free popcorn, some video games, and of course, a full bar.

5 MCDONOUGH'S RESTAURANT & LOUNGE

Directly across Drayton Street from Emporium you see **MCDONOUGH'S RESTAURANT & LOUNGE**. The mere fact that it still refers to itself as a restaurant and lounge will give you an idea of how old school this space is. Though you'd never know it once you walk inside.

McDonough's claim to fame, at least in the last decade plus, is their karaoke bar in the back. Yes, there are certainly other places in Savannah for quality karaoke, but this is widely regarded as the go-to for such shenanigans in the heart of Savannah.

That doesn't mean the food isn't good, because it is. On the menu you will find your usual suspect bar food, of course, but you should know that McDonough's chicken wings are regularly discussed as being some of the best in Savannah. If you are a connoisseur and can't control your desire to find that next great wing, then you should give these a spin. They are available in 8 different flavors and I've loved most of them. Including the buffalo, of course, and their lemon pepper.

When you consider the singing going on over there and the televisions with sports going on over here, late night in here is loud. There's no sugarcoating that. From my seat, though, this is a spot in Savannah where that really doesn't matter. It's a great time.

> **TIP**
>
> **Fancy Parkers** (located on the other side of the Perry Lane Hotel at McDonough Street) is Savannah's centrally located convenience store, featuring a hot food bar 24 hours a day, cold beer to go, and all the other necessities that you will find in your average convenience store.

SOUTH OF FORSYTH CRAWL

1. **THE SENTIENT BEAN,** 13 E. PARK AVE., SAVANNAH, (912) 232-4447, SENTIENTBEAN.COM

2. **BETTY BOMBERS,** 1108 BULL ST., SAVANNAH, (912) 272-9326, BETTYBOMBERS.COM

3. **WHITE WHALE CRAFT ALES,** 1207 BULL ST., SAVANNAH, (912) 358-0724, WHITEWHALECRAFTALES.COM

4. **THE BLACK RABBIT,** 1215 BARNARD ST., SAVANNAH, (912) 200-4940, BLACKRABBITSAV.COM

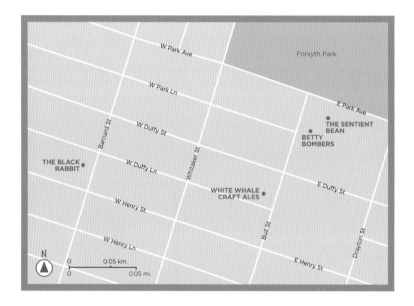

Some may want to call this neighborhood SOFO (South of Forsyth), but it is technically known as Savannah's Victorian District, which was designated as a historic district in 1974.

South of Forsyth

SOFO, Savannah's Only Trendy Nickname

A glance at any map of downtown Savannah will clearly show you that our city was built south from the Savannah River but later developed to surround our largest downtown park, Forsyth Park.

Forsyth Park is roughly 30 acres of beauty in the heart of Savannah. Its central fountain is maybe the most photographed location in town. Just beyond that fountain, you find Collins Quarter at Forsyth, a second location for one of the city's most thriving brunch locales.

But down at the other end of our "Central Park" is a neighborhood that features a tiny cluster of worthwhile eateries and shops. The cluster is anchored by the intersection of Bull Street and Park Avenue, literally at the foot of the park. Technically, it is part of the Savannah Historic Victorian District. But for the sake of our time here together today, it is the neighborhood South of Forsyth. For the record, while the name fits, the nickname has been slow to catch on. Use it sparingly.

TIP

On Saturday mornings this neighborhood is a beehive of activity surrounding Savannah's largest farmers' Market. The Forsyth Farmers' Market runs year-round, except for major holidays, from 9 a.m. until 1 p.m.

1

THE SENTIENT BEAN

Our crawl starts at the corner of Bull Street and Park Avenue. It's a very quiet little corner of town unless it's Saturday morning. That's when the farmers' market is in full swing. Facing the park (north), we turn to the right and walk a hundred or so feet to our first stop, **THE SENTIENT BEAN**.

The "Bean," as it is affectionately known around here, is not only a vegetarian/vegan coffee shop, but it has also served Savannah as a gathering place for artists, musicians, and other creatives looking to bring ideas together for potential growth.

A lot of the art on the walls is for sale. Many of the events they host here benefit social causes. The Sentient Bean is also home to one of Savannah's few "Open Mic Nights," generally held every fourth Tuesday. You are just as likely to see some students here working on an assignment as you are business folks meeting to discuss a major project.

As we said, the food is vegetarian or vegan. Some of it is gluten-free. That has always been the case here at the Sentient Bean. Their offerings have always targeted the vegetarian and vegan crowd, going way back before it was trendy and cool. For that, the Bean is rewarded with a very loyal following in Savannah.

Baked goods fill the case near the counter; the breakfast tacos (both vegetarian and vegan options) are popular as well. The smoothies, coffees, and teas are solid. They even offer a tiny selection of local beers and wine.

The Sentient Bean has been in this spot for almost 20 years. It's hard to believe they weren't the first on the block. But they weren't. Not even close.

Next door, and under the same ownership as the Sentient Bean, is BRIGHTER DAY Natural Foods Deli. Another extremely popular spot at the corner of Bull and Park where our crawl started.

Brighter Day dates back to 1978 here in Savannah. The mission was simple: to offer Savannah natural and organic foods, both as a grocery store and later as a deli. The fully organic deli is open 6 days a week and is Savannah's freshest grab-and-go for organic meals. There is no seating inside. You will have to take that bite to eat and maybe walk it across the street to the park to enjoy on a park bench or picnic table.

The menus change somewhat regularly, but they do offer a great variety of sandwiches, salads, main dishes, and side dishes. Again, all of it organic.

BETTY BOMBERS

Back out at the intersection of Bull and Park, we turn to the south (park at our back) and begin the walk up Bull Street past the takeaway window at Brighter Day and to the next set of stairs about 75 feet ahead. The pale brick building you see is an American Legion Hall Post 135. The building dates back to 1913 and was designed by the same gentleman who designed Savannah's City Hall and Main Public Library.

Take a walk up the steps and inside. Everyone is welcome here. Immediately to the right, you see a doorway to a bar. That is referred to as "the Legion" around here and is one of downtown Savannah's iconic dive bars. We aren't stopping here. Unless, of course, you want to.

Instead, keep walking down the hallway another 25 to 30 feet to the next set of doors. On the right, walking through the doorway, you find an almost literally hidden Savannah gem, BETTY BOMBERS Eatery.

Originally created as an eatery that would cater to the beer-drinking crowd at the bar up front, Betty Bombers has solidified its place in Savannah as some of the best burgers, wings, and sandwiches in the city.

The theme, clearly an homage to World War II, is on display everywhere. In fact, it's not at all uncommon to see vets of many wars gone by in here, enjoying a meal with their families.

They bill themselves as a "no frills" diner. That it most certainly is. You order at the counter and take a number and your food is delivered to your table. My favorite item on the menu here, one that it is almost impossible for me not to

> ### TIP
>
> Local 11ten (1110 Bull St., Savannah, 912-790-9000, local11ten.com) is one of Savannah's better fine dining restaurants. Its rooftop bar, Perch, is small, intimate, and beautiful. It is Savannah's quiet rooftop lounge far away from and several decibels lower than any of the others.

order when I'm stopping in for a bite, is the Ultimate Chicken Sub: grilled chicken, bacon, swiss cheese, lettuce, tomato, pickle, and a basil aioli. It's phenomenal. As are the classic buffalo chicken wings and of course the burgers. All of them. We were reminded of that when we stopped in for photos for this book. Like those wings hot? Try the Reaper, made with Carolina Reaper peppers, some of the hottest peppers in the world. Don't say we didn't warn you.

Don't pass on the milkshakes. The guys went through nearly 3 dozen different ice creams just to land on the perfect milkshake. They are delicious. Then, I think you might be ready for a nap, but we've got crawling to do.

3

WHITE WHALE CRAFT ALES

Back out on Bull Street, turn to the left and continue to the next corner, Duffy Street. At this corner you will find Local 11Ten, one of our better fine dining restaurants.

Diagonally from where you are standing, you will see a row of storefronts. Cross to that corner however you choose. Once there, continue up Bull about 50 feet to our next stop, **WHITE WHALE CRAFT ALES** Beer Market.

White Whale was created by Jason Piccolo, a self proclaimed beer nerd. He wanted to offer Savannah a place to drink carefully curated craft beers without either breaking the bank or fighting the traffic and parking issues you find deeper into the heart of downtown Savannah.

White Whale offers several brews on tap. Beers that you are unlikely to find in too many places here in town. On tap and retail to go as well.

There is also a standing cooler off to one side with what I believe to be one of Savannah's best-kept beer-drinking secrets. Single cans of beer beginning at 3 bucks. The more exclusive the beer, the higher the price for that "loosey" will go.

Regardless, where are you going to find quality beers like this at that price? Not around here you won't. Grab one and have a seat. The staff here is always interested in talking shop.

4

THE BLACK RABBIT

When you wrap up your beer drinking and step back out onto Bull Street, our final destination is 2 short blocks away through one of downtown Savannah's more charming neighborhoods: the Victorian District.

Make your way back to Duffy Street, the direction we came from, and turn left. Continue on Duffy across two cross streets, first Whitaker Street and then Barnard Street. At the corner of Duffy and Barnard look diagonally, and you will see one of Savannah's more unique houses, converted to a home from a church.

Savannah's Victorian District was home to Savannah's "Colored Library," a library created by and for the African American community in the city during segregation. The Carnegie Library is now part of the public library system and is located on Henry Street. Open to the public.

We are going to the left here and about half a block up where you will see a tiny storefront and a few tables outside. Welcome to **THE BLACK RABBIT**.

The Black Rabbit is a lunch counterish pub. Tiny, yes. Maybe a tick more than 30 seats inside but extremely popular with locals. On one side you find the kitchen and the food. On the other is a charming, but as we mentioned tiny, full liquor bar.

The Cuban sandwich is great. As is the Three Piggies featuring Spam, pit ham, sliced pork, aioli, white cheddar, and onion on a bolillo roll. I'm also a big fan of the German potato salad, which carries a nice bite featuring two different onions and mustard.

BULL STREET SOUTH CRAWL

1. **HENNY PENNY ART SPACE AND CAFE,** 1514 BULL ST., SAVANNAH, (912) 328-5497, HENNYPENNYCAFE.COM

2. **BULL STREET TACO,** 1608 BULL ST., SAVANNAH, (912) 349-6931, BULLSTREETTACO.COM

3. **NOM NOM POKE SHOP,** 1821 BULL ST., SAVANNAH, (912) 777-4074, NOMNOMPOKESHOP.COM

4. **FOXY LOXY CAFE,** 1919 BULL ST., SAVANNAH, (912) 401-0543, FOXYLOXYCAFE.COM

5. **BIG BON BODEGA / BIG BON PIZZA,** 2011 BULL ST., SAVANNAH, (912) 349-4847, BIGBONFAMILY.COM

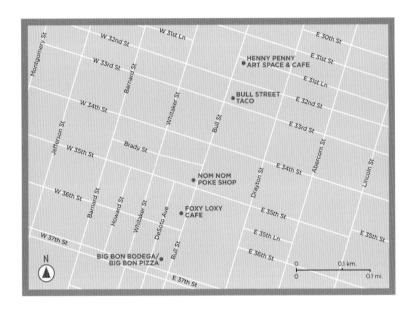

Bull Street South

Savannah's True Local Dining Scene

As we mentioned in our Bull Street North crawl, Bull Street cuts right through the center of our downtown district. It is interrupted only by Forsyth Park. The neighborhood surrounding Bull Street's southern end is a neighborhood very much in transition—for the better, of course. The Starland District has been getting all the headlines as of late with its collection of trendy food and some shopping, and we will visit that in an upcoming crawl.

This is the stretch of Bull Street between Forsyth Park and the Starland District, a neighborhood visited almost exclusively by locals or visitors who dig deep on their homework before they arrive in Savannah, like you.

The stretch is short, only two-tenths of a mile long, but quaint. Along the way, you enjoy a variety of cuisines and Savannah's Main Public Library. The crawl begins at the corner of Bull Street and 31st Lane.

Savannah's Public Library—first established in 1809—was a subscription-based library and the first known library to exist in the state of Georgia.

1 HENNY PENNY ART SPACE AND CAFE

Much like any other city this size, we have a fair share of coffee shops that we can enjoy. We've made a point of sharing only those that were positioned strategically around Savannah during our crawls. Or if they offer something unique. Our first stop on this crawl fits the bill: HENNY PENNY.

It seems every coffee shop out there flexes the same vibe. Students, business folks, hustle, bustle, and tussle. Henny Penny is different in that it caters to parents with kids in tow. Yes, on this side you will find a coffee counter owned by the same folks behind the Coffee Fox and Foxy Loxy, but around the bend you have their art studio.

The art studio is very simply a space where the little ones can play, doodle, draw, paint, you name it. It's their entertainment while Mom and/ or Dad throw back that horchata latte or nitro cold brew. There is more than enough space for a collaboration plus special art project kits they will sell you for $12 so you can spend some time putting them together as a family.

Henny Penny also serves Leopold's Ice Cream without the long lines on Broughton Street. There's a small selection of sandwiches and baked goodies and vegan doughnuts made every day. Definitely a unique space.

While buildings from the Savannah College of Art and Design dot the downtown landscape, Arnold Hall, at Bull Street and 34th, is among its busiest, with students regularly milling about the area and frequenting area eateries.

2

BULL STREET TACO

Exiting onto Bull Street and turning left, you will cross 32nd Street and immediately find yourself approaching our next stop: Bull Street Taco.

BULL STREET TACO is Savannah's hub for Mexican street food. It's the most popular taco by far, and second place isn't even close. It opened a handful of years ago before a lot of this corridor had developed. There were some businesses, of course, but the success of Bull Street Taco guaranteed traffic to the area, which, in turn, fueled even more growth and development.

The food is delicious. Everything you will consume at Bull Street is made on the premises. There are no mixes or shortcuts; there's just made-from-scratch Mexican favorites. The red chili tempura cauliflower taco is a departure from anything you'll find at a traditional taqueria, but it is fantastic. As is the chorizo taco with chipotle crema on a corn tortilla.

The guacamole, which includes lime, achiote oil, and toasted pistachio, is wonderful as well. The margaritas? Well, let's just say you will like everything you drink here. On Mondays those margaritas are 5 bucks all day long.

Bull Street also offers a selection of protein bowls and salads to go along with all the goodness they can offer you. On the weekends you are likely to wait for a table. There is some seating indoors, but a majority of their seats are either outdoors on their patio or out front on the sidewalk.

3

NOM NOM POKE SHOP

Continue out on Bull, southbound; our next stop is a few blocks away. Three to be exact, at the corner of Bull and 35th Street: one of Savannah's few poke shops. When you consider the attention to detail and freshness here, there just aren't too many places in town like it.

For those who aren't familiar, poke is Hawaiian for "slice or chunk"—in this case, raw fish. In particular here at Nom Nom, tuna. The fish is sliced fresh then marinated, usually in soy sauce or an acid, and served in a bowl with rice and vegetables. Bowls of rice and vegetables you can find anywhere. What sets one poke bowl apart from another is the quality and freshness of that fish.

NOM NOM has been open a few years and has enjoyed tremendous success. The key is the freshness, which a lot of places will promise but then underdeliver on. From the day they opened, Nom Nom has been about serving the freshest fish they can find, even if it means not serving any.

If you are stopping in, try their ahi tuna nachos topped with pico, pickled onion, and a creamy togarashi sauce. The Dynamite Tuna Donburi Bowl features pulled ahi tuna, avocado, cucumber, pea shoots, and tempura crunch with two sauces over rice. On the beverage side, it's simple: soda, bottled water, and teas.

4 FOXY LOXY CAFE

Back onto Bull Street, we continue southbound to the middle of the next block and one of Savannah's most popular coffee spots day and night: **FOXY LOXY CAFE.**

Foxy Loxy is the flagship location for a few others we've mentioned already, including the first stop on this crawl, Henny Penny. Are you picking up a pattern?

Foxy has obviously been around the longest and enjoys the greatest following. During the day when school is in session at the Savannah College of Art and Design across the street, you will very likely encounter a line to get to the counter to order a coffee or a bite.

The kolaches—a slightly sweet pastry-like bread filled with sausage, bread, or fruit—are very popular here, as are the tacos. They are delicious. They offer vegetarian and vegan options and a full menu of coffees and signature drinks. I'm partial to the Mexican Mocha here. Made with chocolate, habanero. and cinnamon plus a double shot of espresso and milk.

The house turned coffee shop makes for tight quarters, but there is a courtyard in back that is very popular too. Live music paired with inexpensive beer or bottles of wine—plus a few tacos—make it so.

TIP

If seating inside of Foxy Loxy Cafe gets a little difficult, you can always grab whatever you are enjoying and walk directly across the street to Thomas Square Park and enjoy it in the shade of a tree on the library's grounds.

5 BIG BON BODEGA / BIG BON PIZZA

Exiting Foxy Loxy and continuing down Bull Street, you cross 36th Street. As you do, across the street on the left you see Savannah's Main Public Library. Built in 1916, it was designed by the same gentleman who created Savannah City Hall. In 1963, it was desegregated and joined with the Library for Colored Citizens of Savannah.

The final stop on this crawl is at the end of this block at the corner of Bull and 37th Streets: a Savannah favorite, **BIG BON BODEGA**.

The Big Bon brand was originally created as a food truck offering wood-fired artisan pizzas at a time when Savannah really didn't have a lot of choices in that department. Their success allowed them to evolve into this brick-and-mortar location adjacent to Savannah's blossoming Starland District immediately to the south. Because they had the truck, they didn't offer pizzas here. Instead, they do wood-fired artisan bagels.

Big Bon bagels are not traditional in the sense that you will compare them to your favorite corner spot in Brooklyn, but they are most certainly delicious. The menu features 6 or so flavors of bagels and a handful of bagel sandwiches. You can keep it real with the Pimento Pig (sausage, fried egg, and pimento cream cheese) or swing for the fences with the Bon Mi (roast pork, spicy mayo, pickled carrots and papaya, cucumber, cilantro, and jalapeno). They are all good.

But what about the pizza? Big Bon is also home to some of the best New York–style pies in the city.

Keep in mind, depending on the time of day you are making your way through, you can enjoy some bagels early or pizza late. They are never available at the same time because there is only one oven. Well worth figuring out a way to try both.

The Gingerbread House, located at the corner of Bull and 36th Streets, was built in 1899 and is regarded as an excellent example of "Steamboat Gothic Gingerbread carpentry." It is regularly one of Savannah's most photographed homes and today serves as an event venue and bookstore.

THOMAS SQUARE CRAWL

1. **HOP ATOMICA**, 535 E. 39TH ST., SAVANNAH, (912) 335-2715, HOPATOMICA .COM

2. **AL SALAAM DELI**, 2311 HABERSHAM ST., SAVANNAH, (912) 447-0400, ALSALAAMDELI.COM

3. **GREEN TRUCK NEIGHBORHOOD PUB**, 2430 HABERSHAM ST., SAVANNAH, (912) 234-5885, GREENTRUCKPUB.COM

4. **LONE WOLF LOUNGE**, 2429 LINCOLN ST., SAVANNAH, LONEWOLFSAV.COM

5. **MOODRIGHT'S / OVER YONDER**, 2424 ABERCORN ST., SAVANNAH, (912) 335-7276, MOODRIGHTS.COM / OVERYONDERSAV.COM

6. **ARDSLEY STATION**, 102 E. VICTORY DR., SAVANNAH, (912) 777-5888, ARDSLEYSTATION.COM

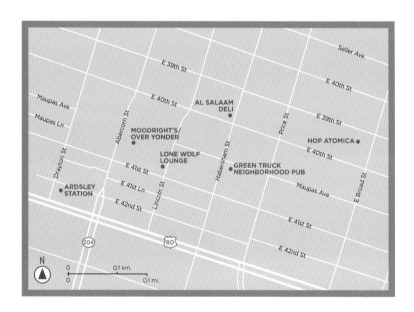

The Thomas Square Streetcar District neighborhood is a National Historic District, created in 1997. Prior to streetcars making it into the area (1888), it was considered Savannah's "southern suburb."

Thomas Square

Our Final "Neighborhood" Crawl

Wrapped into all of Savannah's rich history is a subheader to our city's 200-plus years that not a lot of people talk about. Certainly not as many as you would think, anyway. That's our diversity in architecture. Federal architecture is our oldest and obviously closest to the Savannah River. As you travel south from that point, you can see architectural styles change and evolve to include Georgian style, Gothic Revival, and Victorian. But not everything is centuries old in Savannah. The Thomas Square neighborhood is a good example of that.

TIP

The Thomas Square neighborhood is home to four of Savannah's most popular fine dining restaurants. Elizabeth on 37th, Common Thread, Cotton & Rye, and La Scala are all located within blocks of each other and regularly among Savannah's best.

Thomas Square is one of our most popular "near downtown" neighborhoods. A roughly $10 cab ride from Broughton Street and you find yourself seemingly 100 miles away from the energy of the Historic Landmark District. The neighborhood is home to 10 to 12 of the restaurants most frequented by local Savannah. Some (Big Bon Bodega, Bull Street Taco) have been mentioned in other crawls. But these are some of Savannah's can't-miss places, all within a half mile and 6 blocks of one another.

1

HOP ATOMICA

HOP ATOMICA sets itself apart from the other local breweries in that it is a tiny facility and taproom doing some fantastic beer, seltzers, and spirits. And for the most part you will only find their creations here—located at 39th Street and Broad just outside of the "technical" border of the Thomas Square neighborhood. The sticklers will remind you that Hop is in Baldwin Park, but it still the perfect place to begin a new crawl.

Hop Atomica is a beautiful space featuring nearly 2 dozen flowing taps at any given time. A few are popular enough to be regular features, but the fun here is in trying something you may or may not find here next week. We've enjoyed regular Mexican-style lagers. We've enjoyed blueberry Jolly Rancher sours. And we've enjoyed a whole lot of everything in between. They also distill vodka, rum, and gin on the property as well as a delicious selection of nonalcoholic seltzers.

Hop is also a gastropub, serving pizzas, tacos, and a few other snacks with everything made in-house. Their hummus is outstanding as are some of their brunch offerings. That includes their breakfast pizza topped with sausage, bacon, a runny egg, and mozzarella. I like most of their pies, but that one is some kinda special.

2 AL SALAAM DELI

Standing on 39th Street, we continue our crawl to the left and westbound on 39th Street through a residential neighborhood. You will cross Price Street and continue 1 more block to Habersham Street. At the corner of Habersham and 39th look across the street and slightly to the left at our next stop, **AL SALAAM DELI**.

Al Salaam Deli can best be described as Savannah's favorite Mediterranean greasy spoon. It is every bit that—family owned and operated for nearly two decades in this same spot. I know plenty of people who make a point of stopping by if they are anywhere near here.

The food is delicious and inexpensive, from the crispy but flavorful falafel to the classic lamb or chicken gyros or their hummus. There are a few seats inside. It can get crowded at lunchtime on occasion, but it is also the spot where you are most likely to see the neighborhood coming through in their pajamas for a quick bit of takeout.

3 GREEN TRUCK NEIGHBORHOOD PUB

Stepping back out onto Habersham Street, we turn to the right with our next stop visible a short block away on the left: GREEN TRUCK NEIGHBORHOOD PUB.

Green Truck Pub is to Savannah what Dreamland BBQ is to the state of Alabama, that is, the beginning of nearly every burger conversation in town. Their grass-fed burgers were an instant smash hit almost as soon as they opened their doors over a decade ago.

The secret here is pretty simple. Green Truck has had a philosophy since day one of making everything in-house—including their ketchup. And for many, many years they sported Savannah's best veggie burger—a lot of this city will argue that it still is—also made by hand. Beyond all of that, it's not uncommon to see Green Truck's owner driving away from the local farmers' market on a Saturday morning with the back of his . . . wait for it . . . green truck loaded with as much local produce as they can grab.

There are a lot of ways to go with these burgers. The Trailer Park features pimento cheese and bacon. The Rustico is topped with goat cheese, balsamic caramelized onion, roasted red peppers, and fresh basil.

There's a great selection of local beers on tap and soft drinks as well. Green Truck doesn't accept reservations and there is some outdoor seating.

TIP

The city of Savannah operates a free trolley from near Bay Street beyond Forsyth Park and to the Starland District. It then makes a loop and returns to the heart of downtown. This trolley could cut your travel time to Thomas Square by 80% if you time it right.

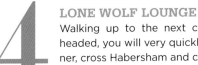

LONE WOLF LOUNGE

Walking up to the next corner in the direction we've been headed, you will very quickly reach 41st Street. Here at this corner, cross Habersham and continue 1 block up to Lincoln Street. When you reach the corner of 41st and Lincoln, you will see a great door with a tiny sign. That's **LONE WOLF LOUNGE**.

If you are keeping score, Lone Wolf Lounge is one of only two true cocktail bars that we've included in our crawls (Artillery Bar being the other in our Bull Street North crawl).

Yes, there have been a couple of dive bars here and there, but only two where you will go to find craftsmanship and true "mixology." That's not at all a slight on any of the bartenders around town; there is a ton of great talent here. But Lone Wolf does what they do very well and very quietly. They've been rewarded for it.

They bill themselves as a neighborhood watering hole, and they very much are. You can find exceptional versions of any classic cocktail here, but I have many times gravitated to the Make Duran Duran Again, featuring electric blue vodka, lavender, and orange blossom. I get a kick out of the British flag they pop into the lemon garnish every single time.

The Thomas Square neighborhood is roughly a half mile from Savannah's Daffin Park and historic Grayson Stadium, one of America's oldest operating baseball stadiums. It opened in 1926 and is currently home to the Savannah Bananas.

5 MOODRIGHT'S / OVER YONDER

Back out on 41st Street, we turn to the right and make our way up the block to Abercorn Street where you find a flower shop. At that corner, turn right, pass two storefronts, and we are at stop number five. A two-for-one stop and a great value: Moodright's and Over Yonder.

MOODRIGHT'S is a warm, comfortable, and inviting bar dressed up to look like a roadside spot in the Midwest somewhere. Paneling, beer lights, and hunting trophies dot the room. There's a pool table and Savannah's only duckpin bowling lanes.

The games will keep you engaged, but the prices will keep you happy. It is one of the downtown area's most affordable venues, featuring a long list of your dad's favorite beers plus some craft brews. But that's not all.

To the left as you enter the room is a hallway that looks like it is headed to the restrooms, and it does. But if you make your way through that hallway all the way to the back, you've a whole other set of circumstances and fun.

OVER YONDER is the separately branded back room at Moodright's. It's home to their kitchen, which features one of the best no-frills burgers in town. The french fries back here alone are a draw. You can get 'em topped with cowboy ranch and bacon aioli.

The cocktails are very creative too. Wrangler Butt anyone? Rye, Fernet, Campari, and Cheerwine. Or maybe Cool Ranch Water featuring tequila, Topo Chico, cactus juice, and lime juice.

There's a great vibe back here and a small stage for live music. When the weather is cooperating, the garage door in the back slides open, giving a peek at the residential neighborhood behind the bar. Around here, it doesn't get much more local than this.

6 ARDSLEY STATION

Once again, you return out to Abercorn to begin the short walk to our final stop on the crawl. Back at the corner of Abercorn and 41st, continue along Abercorn to the next corner, 42nd Street. About 50 feet to the left is one of Savannah's cooking schools and kitchen supply stores, Chef Darin's Kitchen Table. It is a beautiful facility and worthy of your time if you have some. But our next stop is to the right and across Abercorn Street.

Continuing up 42nd Street, you won't see a restaurant up ahead. Trust us. It is just ahead on the left. When you reach the next cross street, Drayton Street, you've arrived. You'll see the courtyard for **ARDSLEY STATION** on your left.

If the rustic vibe at our two stops didn't fit your bill, Ardsley Station most certainly will. It sits at the corner of Victory Drive and Drayton Street, which makes it something of "the beginning" of the area to the north a lot of locals refer to as "downtown Savannah."

The bar is small, roughly six seats, but the dining room is beautiful and airy with glass surrounding it. And as you already saw, there is plenty of outdoor seating and even a couple of televisions out there to take in a ball game.

The food is simple, nothing complicated or difficult to pronounce. Crab cakes, a great burger, steak frites, or maybe some classic Savannah chicken and waffles with cheddar, scallions, and maple syrup. They have a good wine list by the glass and delicious cocktails as well. The Snoop and Dr. Drayton featuring gin, pamplemousse, basil, grapefruit, and lime is a crowd favorite—if not for the quality of the beverage, then certainly for the name.

STARLAND DISTRICT CRAWL

1. **THE VAULT KITCHEN AND MARKET,** 2112 BULL ST., SAVANNAH, (912) 201-1950, THEVAULTKITCHEN.COM

2. **SQUIRREL'S PIZZA,** 2218 BULL ST., SAVANNAH, (912) 335-7873, SQUIRRELSPIZZA.COM

3. **UKIYO SAVANNAH,** 2224 BULL ST., SAVANNAH, (912) 428-5683

4. **TWO TIDES BREWING COMPANY,** 12 W. 41ST ST., SAVANNAH, (912) 667-0706, TWOTIDESBREWING.COM

5. **SUPERBLOOM,** 2418 DESOTO AVE., SAVANNAH, (912) 452-0106, SUPERBLOOMSAV.COM

6. **PIZZERIA VITTORIA NAPOLETANA,** 2411 DESOTO AVE., SAVANNAH, (912) 417-3002, VITTORIAPIZZERIA.COM

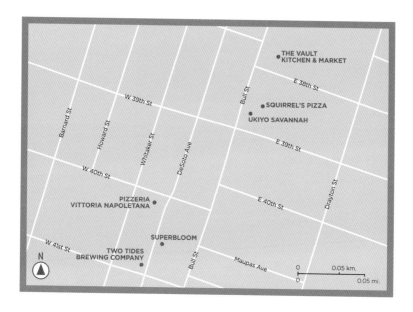

The Starland District hosts a regular First Friday event outside of warmer summer months. It features art exhibitions, street fairs, and music. You can find more information closer to your visit on Facebook: "First Fridays in Starland."

Starland District

Savannah's "Next Big Thing"

In 1932, a dairy opened in Savannah at the corner of Bull Street and 41st. The Starland Dairy supplied milk to a lot of Savannah until the 1980s. In 1999, two graduates from the Savannah College of Art and Design with degrees in historic preservation set out to attempt to revitalize this section of downtown Savannah with the since abandoned dairy as a centerpiece.

The vision was to create a neighborhood haven for artists and creatives in a variety of ways. Food, art, and music were just the beginning. By 2001, 40 professional artists were working in this neighborhood.

In the last half decade or so, the Starland District has solidified its place as Savannah's next big thing. The Bull Street corridor has been an attraction for years now. In the last half decade or so, however, development (and redevelopment) has begun to make its way into the side streets. It is why many newcomers to Savannah are looking to live here.

People want to live here, of course, because of the options they will find for nighttime entertainment a short walk away. The Starland District has grown into something of a local's version of downtown Savannah. Parking is easier, crowds are smaller, and, in a lot of cases, the food is better than anything you will find closer to the riverfront. Which allows us to give it the nickname Savannah's next big thing.

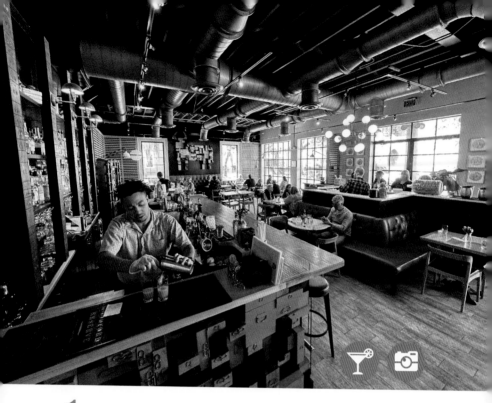

1

THE VAULT KITCHEN AND MARKET

Our crawl begins very near the end of our Bull Street South crawl and the very popular Big Bon Bodega. Once you cross 37th Street, you begin to enter the heart of Savannah's Starland District. One block up at 38th Street you find our first stop: **THE VAULT KITCHEN AND MARKET.**

The Vault is very popular with local Savannah folks for a couple of reasons. First, it has its own parking lot adjacent, which makes business lunches a snap to get in and out of, but it also has consistently good food. Built in what was formerly a bank building, hence the name, the Vault offers Asian-inspired fare including noodle bowls, dumplings, and sushi.

I'm a big fan of their Chicken Claypot, featuring tender chunks of chicken, herbs, curry Thai chili, ginger, and Thai green eggplants. The broth is rich and delicious and served with a side of white rice. If you are looking to snack, their sushi is a go-to for a lot of Savannah, but you won't be mistaking it for the heart of Tokyo. For beverages, I'd consider the Bonnie and Clyde: gin, fresh strawberry smash, and Jack Rudy small batch tonic.

2 SQUIRREL'S PIZZA

A very short walk across 38th Street, you will begin to enter the heart of the Starland District. Your initial introduction is our next stop, which you will come up on almost immediately on your left: SQUIRREL'S PIZZA.

Pizza is a thing in the Starland District. It wasn't all that long ago that we had none. That created something of a race to fill the void not only around here but in Savannah in general. One of the shops that came to be is Squirrel's Pizza.

At a glance, you will assume that Squirrel's is a traditional Neapolitan-style pizza, and in many ways it is. But what makes this slightly different is they add a tiny crunch more common to a Tonda Romana. The variation makes for a wonderful pie. Of course you can opt for traditional toppings, but don't overlook the Benny Blanco: mozzarella, parmesan, rosemary, and Agrumato lemon extra-virgin olive oil. Looking for a unique cocktail from their full liquor bar? Go for the Moonlight in Georgia: rye whiskey, Amaro, lemon, and a handmade clove and blood orange syrup.

3 UKIYO SAVANNAH

Pizza behind us (for now), immediately next door to Squirrel's you will see Water Witch, one of Savannah's tiki bars. If fruity rum drinks are your thing, that's for you. Our next stop, though, is two more doors down at the corner of Bull and 39th Streets: a Japanese street food paradise called **UKIYO**.

Stick with us here, but Ukiyo is Savannah's izakaya, a Japanese word for an informal bar that serves snacks. You may prefer "pub" because it's easier to pronounce, but either way this is where we are.

Owned by the same group behind the Collins Quarter (Bull Street North crawl), Ukiyo is the vision of its Australian owner who spent nearly two decades in Japan. Simply put, he loves the food, he loves the vibe. He then believed it was time to bring it to Savannah's edgy Starland District.

The menu is difficult to pin down. Sure, you will find charred edamame. Of course you will find grilled skewers, but the fun here lies beyond all of that with dishes like salt and pepper quail or a bowl of duck ramen. Behind the bar, you will find an impressive selection of Japanese whiskeys, plus the usual suspects, of course.

4 TWO TIDES BREWING COMPANY

We've taken in a lot in a very short space, but trust us when we tell you there is a much more to the Starland District. Looking directly across the street you see the Wormhole, a very popular late-night and live music venue in Savannah.

Continuing southbound on Bull across 39th you will cross Bull Street at 40th and walk toward Savannah's legendary Back in the Day Bakery (see sidebar above). Continue your walk to the left and down Bull Street; you will pass a tattoo parlor and a veterinary clinic. The next corner is 41st Street. If you look up, you will see the famous Starland Dairy we mentioned to you at the top of the crawl. Around the corner on 41st, our next stop is about 150 feet ahead: **TWO TIDES BREWING COMPANY**.

Two Tides is one of Savannah's most popular breweries, and that is saying something. The other two breweries that draw the most attention are located deeper into downtown Savannah. This location for Two Tides makes it an ideal spot for locals looking for great craft beers, which they obviously are.

The taproom is upstairs (there is no elevator) in a renovated old house. Old house around here means several rooms, some a smidgen on the small side. If it isn't too crowded, there is plenty of space for everyone. We make a point of singling this out only because many times the thought of a brewery evokes visions of a large warehouse space. This is far cozier and inviting of conversation. It's just one of the things that makes Two Tides unique.

As you might imagine, the selection of beers is regularly on the move. It's a working brewery with the goods created downstairs. Enjoy one or a few and save time for Savannah's smallest bar, which you will find down the stairs and around the bend, but in the same building. It's called Smol and offers some of Two Tides beers plus a selection of seltzer-based cocktails and mocktails.

5

SUPERBLOOM

Stepping back out onto DeSoto Avenue from Smol, if you stopped there, looking across the lane, our next stop is impossible to miss. Superbloom is one of Savannah's best-kept secrets and proof that this crawl isn't only about alcohol.

SUPERBLOOM is an artists' collaborative and coffee shop. It was founded back in 2016 when they occupied a small space nearby before moving into this location here on DeSoto Avenue.

Superbloom offers some of Savannah's most unique shopping, carrying items from nearly three dozen local artists. The items you find here you are unlikely to see anywhere else. The selection is curated beautifully.

The draw on a food crawl is their drink counter. Superbloom offers a fantastic selection of superfood lattes, including tea and coffee beverages, plus kombucha and clean wines. All of their drinks are gluten- and dairy-free. They include selections like Lavender Rose or a Red Bean Vanilla Matcha or a Salted Maple. They also offer more mainstream coffees, including espresso.

All the drinks are made right in front of you and in a majority of cases way too pretty to want to drink. See for yourself.

> Savannah's first dog park was created next door to the Starland Cafe on 41st Street between Bull and Drayton Streets.

In an increasingly territorial city, the Starland District doesn't really believe in perfectly defined borders. Instead, Starland's founders accept that the true Starland District is made up from small pieces of every designated neighborhood surrounding its central corridor, Bull Street.

6 PIZZERIA VITTORIA NAPOLETANA

Standing back out in the middle of DeSoto Avenue, you can clearly see a fence ahead of you dividing DeSoto Avenue from a very large beer garden. That is Savannah's very popular food truck park. It is called Starland Yard. You can access it a few feet away from DeSoto Avenue.

The food trucks rotate daily through the yard, but there is one permanent food outlet that in 3 short years has become a Savannah icon: **PIZZERIA VITTORIA**.

Headed up by chef/owner Kyle Jacovino, Pizzeria Vittoria has drawn national attention to what he has created here in this little corner of Savannah. Yes, the pizza is that great.

The perfect pizza is an obsession with Kyle. His creations regularly involve Southern influences with modern twists. The pies and the sometimes 45-minute-plus wait to grub on the weekend speak for themselves.

Beyond a traditional classic margherita, mozzarella, marinara, and basil, the Lorraine is maybe their most popular. It is with me anyway. A beautiful leopard-spotted pie topped with meatball, ricotta, Calabrian chilies, marinara, and mozzarella. The ingredients are the best they can get their hands on. The proof is in every bite.

Vittoria also features a rotating daily pie special, plus a smallish list of grinders and salads. All of it delicious.

The beverages come from the large bar you will see in the middle of the food truck park. Having received a wristband in order to enter the park, you will pay for everything once when you are ready to leave.

Four eateries we did not mention on this crawl deserve your attention. These places all keep day hours only: Troupial Cafe (9 W. 43rd St., Savannah, 912-441-0596, streetfoodhomeflavors.com; open Tuesday to Sunday 9 a.m. to 5 p.m.); Starland Cafe (11 E. 41st St., Savannah, 912-443-9355, thestarlandcafe.com; open Monday to Friday 11 a.m. to 3 p.m.); Trick's BBQ (2601 Bull St., Savannah, 910-631-0100, facebook.com/TricksBBQ; open Tuesday to Saturday 11:30 a.m. to 5 p.m.); and Back in the Day Bakery (2403 Bull St., Savannah, 912-495-9292, backinthedaybakery.com/back-in-the-day-bakery; open Saturday and Sunday 10 a.m. to 3 p.m.).

Rooftop Appendix

BAR JULIAN
201 PORT STREET AT THE THOMPSON HOTEL, SAVANNAH, GA 31401,
(912) 790-1234, BARJULIAN.COM

DRAYTON HOTEL
7 DRAYTON STREET AT BAY STREET, SAVANNAH, GA 31401, (912) 662-8900,
THEDRAYTONHOTEL.COM

ELECTRIC MOON
400 WEST RIVER STREET AT JW MARRIOTT HOTEL, SAVANNAH, GA 31401,
(912) 373-9100, PLANTRIVERSIDE.COM

THE GROVE
301 WEST CONGRESS STREET, SAVANNAH, GA 31401, (912) 777-7597

THE LOST SQUARE AT THE ALIDA HOTEL
412 WILLIAMSON STREET, SAVANNAH, GA 31401, (912) 715-7000,
THEALIDAHOTEL.COM

MYRTLE AND ROSE
400 WEST RIVER STREET AT JW MARRIOTT HOTEL, SAVANNAH, GA 31401,
(912) 373-9100, PLANTRIVERSIDE.COM

PERCH
1110 BULL STREET, SAVANNAH, GA 31401, (912) 790-9000, LOCAL11TEN.COM

PEREGRIN AT THE PERRY LANE HOTEL
256 EAST PERRY STREET, SAVANNAH, GA 31401, (912) 415-9000

ROCKS ON THE ROOF
102 WEST BAY STREET AT THE BOHEMIAN HOTEL, SAVANNAH, GA 31401,
(912) 721-3901, KESSLERCOLLECTION.COM

SORRY CHARLIE'S
116 WEST CONGRESS STREET, SAVANNAH, GA 31401, (912) 234-5397,
SORRYCHARLIES.COM

TOP DECK AT THE COTTON SAIL HOTEL
126 WEST BAY STREET, SAVANNAH, GA 31401, (912) 200-3700, HILTON.COM

VICI ROOFTOP
411 WEST CHARLTON STREET, SAVANNAH, GA 31401, VICIROOFTOP.COM

Worth the Drive Appendix

FINCHES SANDWICHES AND SUNDRIES
2600 MECHANICS AVENUE, THUNDERBOLT, GA (912) 509-8053.
FINCHESSANDWICHES.SHOPSETTINGS.COM

ROCKY'S NY DELI AND CATERING
7360 SKIDAWAY ROAD, SAVANNAH, GA 31406, (912) 354-2914,
ROCKYSOFSAVANNAH.COM

SUNDAE CAFÉ
304 1ST STREET, TYBEE ISLAND, GA 31328, (912) 786-7694, SUNDAECAFE.COM

SEA WOLF TYBEE ISLAND
106 CAMPBELL AVENUE, TYBEE ISLAND, GA 31328, SEAWOLFTYBEE.COM

SANDFLY BBQ
8413 FERGUSON AVENUE, SAVANNAH, GA 31406, (912) 356-5463,
SANDFLYBBQ.COM

THE WYLD DOCK BAR
2740 LIVINGSTON AVENUE, SAVANNAH, GA 31406, (912) 692-1219,
THEWYLDDOCKBAR.COM

Index

Photo Credits

All photos by Jesse Blanco except the following:

208 Wine Bar: pp. 31, 32
1540 Room: p. 118
Ardsley Station: pp. 166, 167
Artillery Bar: p. 101
Baobab: p. 1
Big Bon Pizza: pp. 154, 155
Black Rabbit: pp. 142, 143
Bull Street Taco: pp. 148, 149
Café M: p. 30
Chia Chong Photography: pp. i, iii, 2, 3, 4
Chocolat by Adam Turoni: p. 54
The Collins Quarter: pp. 96, 97
Crystal Beer Parlor: p. 110
Daniel Reed Hospitality: pp. 116, 117
Foxy Loxy: p. 153
The Gaslight Group: p. 33
Green Truck Pub: p. 162
The Grove: pp. 42, 43
Hop Atomica: pp. 158, 159
Java Burrito: p. 75
JW Marriott Savannah: pp. 5, 6, 8, 9
Kayak Kafe: pp. 66, 67
Leopold's Ice Cream: pp. 73, 74
Lone Wolf Lounge: p. 163
Melissa Marcarelli Photography: pp. 118, 138, 164
Mirabelle: pp. 120, 121
Nom Nom Poke Shop: pp. 150, 151
The Ordinary Pub: pp. 58, 59
Rancho Alegre: p. 78
Repeal 33: pp. 80, 81
Somi Benson-Jaja: p. 128
Sorry Charlie's: p. 39
Squirrel's Pizza: pp. 171, 172
Superbloom: pp. 176, 177
Tequila's Town: p. 91
Thompson Hotel Savannah: pp. 34, 35
Treylor Park Restaurants: pp. 28, 29

Acknowledgments

FOR YEARS I HAVE TOLD ANYONE INTERESTED IN LISTENING that starting and growing a business from scratch is the hardest thing I will ever do simply because if something harder comes along, I'm not doing it. Yet here we are over a decade later, chronicling Savannah and the Low Country's food scene. Eating for a living. Yes, I am the luckiest man in the world.

Of course, none of this has happened in a vacuum. The list of people and characters who have helped—and many times carried us—along the way would be long enough to fill a novel. I wish I could say I don't know where to begin to say thank you, but I most certainly do.

My becoming a food writer was Senea Crystal's idea. She not only planted the seed back in 2010, but was critical to the brand's creation and initial growth. None of this would have been possible without her vision and passion to help make it happen.

To my dear friend Monique Cabrera, who was calling shots on this journey 5-plus years in advance. I was better prepared to handle life as an entrepreneur because of that. It's been so critical. Thank you. Also, to my friends Michael Owens and Joe Marinelli for the crutch as we limped along trying to make sense of it all.

A huge thank-you to everyone at Globe Pequot for the faith and trust to document Savannah's food scene for you.

To my tribe: Tara Parker, Lauren Dasher Blanco, Amanda Cifaldi, Dawn Harris, Jennifer Wielgoszinski, Enocha Edenfield, and my sister Sandy. I'm probably still bumping into walls without your unwavering support.

Finally and most importantly, of course, to my beautiful wife Sheila and daughter Alexandra. There aren't enough thank-yous to share for your allowing me to pursue a dream. You are both my entire world and I am nothing without your love and support. At least you get to eat well, right?

About the Author

JESSE BLANCO is, without question, one of Savannah's most recognizable media personalities. His laid-back style and ability to connect with viewers and readers remain his calling card following a 24-year career in television news.

During his 5 years as a news anchor at the local FOX affiliate, Jesse always found creative ways to connect with his audience. That talent extended to his weekly food column in the *Savannah Morning News*, which very quickly became one of that publication's most popular features between 2012 and 2018.

Over that 24-year career in TV news, Jesse lived in Florida, Nashville, and El Paso, Texas, covering anything from major sporting events to space shuttle launches and presidential inaugurations.

In 2010, Jesse and his business partner created a blog and later a television show dedicated to the underappreciated side of Savannah's food scene. Four years later, Savannah's food scene exploded and his brand Eat It and Like It found itself sitting in the front row to witness it all.

Since 2014 he's been the Savannah area's only full-time food writer.

Jesse was born in California but calls Miami, Florida, his hometown, having been raised in a very large Cuban American family where the genetic makeup consists of food, music, dancing, laughing, and friendship. Throw in an insatiable desire to travel and explore and you get someone who is only happy learning or trying new things.

Jesse is married with one child.